An Authentic Narrative of Some Remarkable and Interesting Particulars in the Life of
****

AN
AUTHENTIC NARRATIVE,

OF SOME

Remarkable and Interesting Particulars

IN THE

LIFE of ✱✱✱✱✱✱✱✱. *Rev. J. Newton*

Communicated

In a SERIES of LETTERS,

TO

The REVEREND Mr HAWEIS,
Rector of Aldwinckle, Northamptonshire;

And by him (at the Request of Friends) now made public.

I will bring the blind by a way that they knew not; I will lead them in paths that they have not known; I will make darkness light before them, and crooked things straight. These things will I do unto them, and not forsake them. Isa. xlii. 16.

I am as a wonder unto many. Psal. lxxi. 7.

The THIRD EDITION.

LONDON:
Printed for S. DRAPIER, T. HITCH, and P. HILL.
M.DCC.LXV.

PREFACE.

THE first of the following Letters is so well adapted an introduction to the rest, that to trouble the reader with a long preface would be quite needless and impertinent. I will therefore detain him from entering upon the delightful and instructive relation which the following sheets present him with, little longer, than while I assure him that the narrative is quite ge-

PREFACE.

nuine, and that the following letters were written to me at my requeſt. Some verbal relations of the facts awakened my curioſity to ſee a more connected account of them, which the author very obligingly conſented to, having at that time no intention of its being made public.—But the repeated ſollicitations of friends have at laſt prevailed; and indeed the publication is the more needful, as ſeveral imperfect copies have been handed about, and there has been cauſe to think ſome ſurreptitious edition might ſteal through the preſs into the hands of the public.

I have therefore, with conſent of the author, now ſent theſe letters

PREFACE.

ters abroad in their original form. They were written in haste, as letters of friendship, to gratify my curiosity; but the style, as well as the narrative itself, is so plain and easy, that corrections were thought needless. I can only add my best wishes, that the great truths they contain may prove as edifying, as the facts are striking and entertaining.

T. HAWEIS.

Aldwinckle,
Aug. 1764.

LETTER I.

Reverend and dear Sir,

I Make no doubt but you have at times had pleasing reflections upon that promise made to the Israelites, *Deut.* viii. 2. They were then in the wilderness, surrounded with difficulties, which were greatly aggravated by their own distrust and perverseness: they had experienced a variety of dispensations, the design of which they could not as yet understand; they frequently lost sight of God's gracious purposes in their favour, and were much discouraged by reason of the way. To compose and animate their minds, Moses here suggests to them, that there was a future happy time drawing near, when

their

their journey and warfare should be finished; that they should soon be put in possession of the promised land, and have rest from all their fears and troubles; and then it would give them pleasure to look back upon what they now found so uneasy to bear—" Thou shalt remember all the way " by which the Lord thy God led thee " through this wilderness."

But the importance and comfort of these words is still greater, if we consider them in a spiritual sense, as addressed to all who are passing through the wilderness of this world to a heavenly Canaan; who, by faith in the promises and power of God, are seeking an eternal rest in that kingdom which cannot be shaken. The hope of that glorious inheritance inspires us with some degree of courage and zeal to press forward to where JESUS has already entered as our forerunner; and when our eye is fixed upon him, we are more than conquerors over all that would withstand our progress. But we have not yet attained: we still feel the infirmities of a fallen nature: through the remains of ignorance and unbelief, we often mistake the Lord's dealings with us, and are ready to complain, when, if we

knew

knew all, we should rather rejoice. But to us likewise there is a time coming, when our warfare shall be accomplished, our views enlarged, and our light increased: then with what transports of adoration and love shall we look back upon the way by which the Lord led us! We shall then see and acknowledge, that mercy and goodness directed every step; we shall see that what our ignorance once called adversities and evils, were in reality blessings, which we could not have done well without: that nothing befel us without a cause; that no trouble came upon us sooner, or pressed us more heavily, or continued longer, than our case required: in a word, that our many afflictions were each in their place among the means employed by divine grace and wisdom, to bring us to the possession of that exceeding and eternal weight of glory, which the Lord has prepared for his people. And even in this imperfect state, though we are seldom able to judge aright of our present circumstances, yet if we look upon the years of our past life, and compare the dispensations we have been brought through, with the frame of our minds under each successive

period;

period; if we consider how wonderfully one thing has been connected with another, so that what we now number amongst our greatest advantages, perhaps, took their first rise from incidents which we thought hardly worth our notice; and that we have sometimes escaped the greatest dangers that threatned us, not by any wisdom or foresight of our own, but by the intervention of circumstances which we neither desired or thought of—I say, when we compare and consider these things by the light afforded us in the holy Scripture, we may collect indisputable proof, from the narrow circle of our own concerns, that the wise and good providence of God watches over his people from the earliest moment of their life, over-rules and guards them through all their wanderings in a state of ignorance, leads them in a way that they know not, till at length his providence and grace concur in those events and impressions, which bring them to the knowledge of Him and themselves.

I am persuaded that every believer will, upon due reflection, see enough in his own case to confirm this remark; but not all in the same degree. The outward circumstances

stances of many have been uniform, they have known but little variety in life; and with respect to their inward change, it has been effected in a secret way, unnoticed by others, and almost unperceived by themselves — The Lord has spoken to them, not in thunder and tempest, but with a still small voice he has drawn them gradually to himself; so that though they have a happy assurance of the thing, that they know and love him, and are passed from death unto life; yet of the precise time and manner, they can give little account. Others he seems to select, in order to shew the exceeding riches of his grace, and the greatness of his mighty power; he suffers the natural rebellion and wickedness of their hearts to have full scope; while sinners of less note are cut off with little warning, these are spared, though sinning with a high hand, and as it were studying their own destruction. At length, when all that knew them are perhaps expecting to hear that they are made signal instances of divine vengeance, the Lord (whose thoughts are high above ours, as the heavens are higher than the earth) is pleased to pluck them as brands out of the fire,

and

and to make them monuments of his mercy, for the encouragement of others: they are, beyond expectation, convinced, pardoned, and changed. A case of this sort indicates a divine power no less than the creation of a world: it is evidently the Lord's doing, and it is marvellous in the eyes of all those who are not blinded by prejudice and unbelief.

Such was the persecuting Saul: his heart was full of enmity against JESUS of Nazareth, and therefore he persecuted and made havoc of his disciples. He had been a terror to the church of Jerusalem, and was going to Damascus with the same views——— He was yet breathing out threatnings and slaughter against all that loved the Lord JESUS———He thought little of the mischief he had hitherto done—He was engaged for the suppression of the whole sect; and hurrying from house to house, from place to place, he carried menaces in his look, and repeated threatnings with every breath. Such was his spirit and temper, when the Lord JESUS, whom he hated and opposed, checked him in the height of his rage, called this bitter persecutor to the honour of an apostle, and inspired him with great

zeal

zeal and earnestness, to preach the faith, which he so lately destroyed.

Nor are we without remarkable displays of the same sovereign efficacious grace in our own times——I may particularly mention the instance of the late Colonel Gairdner. If any real satisfaction could be found in a sinful course, he would have met with it; for he pursued the experiment with all possible advantages—He was habituated to evil; and many uncommon, almost miraculous deliverances, made no impression upon him. Yet *he* likewise was made willing in the day of God's power: and the bright example of his life, illustrated and diffused by the account of him published since his death, has afforded an occasion of much praise to God, and much comfort to his people.

After the mention of such names, can you permit me, Sir, to add *my own?* If I do, it must be with a very humbling distinction. These once eminent sinners, proved eminent Christians: much had been forgiven them, they loved much. St Paul could say, " The grace bestowed upon me " was not in vain; for I laboured more " abundantly than they all." Colonel

B   Gairdner

Gairdner likewise was as a city set upon an hill, a burning and a shining light; the manner of his conversion was hardly more singular, than the whole course of his conversation from that time to his death. Here, alas, the parallel greatly fails ! it has not been thus with me—I must take deserved shame to myself, that I have made very unsuitable returns for what I have received. But if the question is only concerning the patience and long-suffering of God, the wonderful interposition of his providence in favour of an unworthy sinner, the power of his grace in softening the hardest heart, and the riches of his mercy in pardoning the most enormous and aggravated transgressions; in these respects I know no case more extraordinary than my own. And indeed most persons, to whom I have related my story, have thought it worthy of being preserved.

I never gave any succinct account in writing, of the Lord's dealing with me, till very lately; for I was deterred on the one hand by the great difficulty of writing properly when *Self* is concerned; on the other, by the ill use which persons of corrupt and perverse minds are often known to make
of

of such instances. The Psalmist reminds us, that a reserve in these things is proper, when he says, "Come unto me, all you "*that fear God*, and I will tell you what "he hath done for my soul;" and our Lord cautions us not to "cast pearls be-"fore swine." The pearls of a Christian are, perhaps, his choice experiences of the Lord's power and love in the concerns of his soul; and these should not be at all adventures made public, lest we give occasion to earthly and groveling souls, to profane what they cannot understand. These were the chief reasons of my backwardness; but a few weeks since I yielded to the judgment and request of a much respected friend, and sent him a relation at large, in a series of eight letters. The event has been what I little expected; I wrote to one person, but my letters have fallen into many hands: amongst others, I find they have reached your notice; and instead of blaming me for being too tedious and circumstantial, which was the fault I feared I had committed, you are pleased to desire a still more distinct detail. As you and others of my friends apprehend my compliance with this request may be attended

with

with some good effect, may promote the pleasing work of praise to our adorable Redeemer, or confirm the faith of some or other of his people, I am willing to obey: I give up my own reasonings upon the inexpediency of so inconsiderable a person as myself adventuring in so public a point of view. If God may be glorified on my behalf, and his children in any measure comforted or instructed, by what I have to declare of his goodness, I shall be satisfied; and am content to leave all other possible consequences of this undertaking in his hands, who does all things well.

I must again have recourse to my memory, as I retained no copies of the letters you saw. So far as I can recollect what I then wrote, I will relate, but shall not affect a needless variety of phrase and manner, merely because those have been already perused by many. I may perhaps in some places, when repeating the same facts, express myself in nearly the same words; yet I propose, according to your desire, to make this relation more explicit and particular than the former, especially towards the close, which I wound up hastily, lest my friend should be wearied. I hope you
will

will likewise excuse me, if I do not strictly confine myself to narration, but now and then intersperse such reflections as may offer while I am writing; and though you have signified your intentions of communicating what I send you to others, I must not on this account affect a conciseness and correctness, which is not my natural talent, lest the whole should appear dry and constrained. I shall therefore (if possible) think only of you, and write with that confidence and freedom which your friendship and candour deserve. This sheet may stand as a preface; and I purpose, as far as I can, to intermit many other engagements, until I have compleated the task you have assigned me. In the mean time I entreat the assistance of your prayers, that in this, and all my poor attempts, I may have a single eye to his glory, who was pleased to call me out of horrid darkness into the marvellous light of his gospel.

I am, with sincere respect,

Dear Sir,

Your obliged and affectionate Servant.

January, 12th 1763.

LETTER II.

Reverend Sir,

I CAN sometimes feel a pleasure in repeating the grateful acknowledgment of David, "O Lord, I am thy servant, "the son of thine handmaid; thou hast "loosed my bands." The tender mercies of God towards me, were manifested in the first moment of my life——I was born as it were in his house, and dedicated to him in my infancy. My mother (as I have heard from many) was a pious experienced Christian; she was a Dissenter, in communion with the late Dr Jennings. I was her only child; and as she was of a weak constitution and a retired temper, almost her whole employment was the care of my education. I have some faint remembrance of her care and instructions. At a time when I could not be more than three years of age, she herself taught me English, and with so much success, (as I had something of a forward turn), that when I was four years old, I could read with propriety in any common book that offered.

ed. ' She stored my memory, which was then very retentive, with many valuable pieces, chapters, and portions of scripture, catechisms, hymns, and poems. My temper at that time seemed quite suitable to her wishes: I had little inclination to the noisy sports of children, but was best pleased when in her company, and always as willing to learn as she was to teach me. How far the best education may fall short of reaching the heart, will strongly appear in the sequel of my history: yet I think, for the encouragement of pious parents to go on in the good way, of doing their part faithfully to form their childrens minds, I may properly propose myself as an instance. Though in process of time I sinned away all the advantages of these early impressions, yet they were for a great while a restraint upon me; they returned again and again, and it was very long before I could wholly shake them off; and when the Lord at length opened my eyes, I found a great benefit from the recollection of them. Further, my dear mother, besides the pains she took with me, often commended me with many prayers and tears

tears to God, and I doubt not but I reap the fruits of these prayers to this hour.

My mother observed my early progress with peculiar pleasure, and intended from the first to bring me up with a view to the ministry, if the Lord should so incline my heart. In my sixth year I began to learn Latin; but before I had time to know much about it, the intended plan of my education was broke short.——The Lord's designs were far beyond the views of an earthly parent: he was pleased to reserve me for an unusual proof of his patience, providence, and grace; and therefore over-ruled the purpose of my friends, by depriving me of this excellent parent, when I was something under seven years old. I was born the 24th July 1725, and she died the 11th of that month, 1732.

My father was then at sea, (he was a commander in the Mediterranean trade at that time): he came home the following year, and soon after married again. Thus I passed into different hands. I was well treated in all other respects; but the loss of my mother's instructions was not repaired. I was now permitted to mingle with careless and profane children, and soon began

gan to learn their ways. Soon after [my] father's marriage I was sent to a boardin[g] school in Essex, where the imprudent se[ve]rity of the master almost broke my spi[rit] and relish for books. With him I forg[ot] the first principles and rules of arithmet[ic] which my mother had taught me years [be]fore. I staid there two years: in the l[ast] of the two, a new usher coming, who [ob]served and suited my temper, I took to [the] Latin with great eagerness; so that bef[ore] I was ten years old, I reached and ma[in]tained the first post in the second cla[ss] which in that school read *Tully* and *Vir[gil]*. I believe I was pushed forward too fast, a[nd] therefore not being grounded, I soon l[ost] all I had learned, (for I left school in [my] tenth year); and when I long afterwa[rds] undertook the Latin language from boo[ks] I think I had little if any advantage fr[om] what I had learned before.

My father's second marriage was from [a] family in Essex; and when I was elev[en] years old, he took me with him to sea. [He] was a man of remarkable good sense, a[nd] great knowledge of the world; he to[ok] great care of my morals, but could [not] supply my mother's part. Having be[en] educat[ed] educated himself in Spain, he always observed an air of distance and severity in his carriage, which overawed and discouraged my spirit. I was always in fear when before him, and therefore he had the less influence. From that time to the year 1742 I made several voyages, but with considerable intervals between, which were chiefly spent in the country, excepting a few months in my fifteenth year, when I was placed upon a very advantageous prospect at Alicant in Spain; but my unsettled behaviour, and impatience of restraint, rendered that design abortive.

In this period, my temper and conduct were exceedingly various. At school, or soon after, I had little concern about religion, and easily received very ill impressions. But I was often disturbed with convictions; I was fond of reading from a child; among other books, *Bennet's christian Oratory* often came in my way; and though I understood but little of it, the course of life therein recommended appeared very desirable, and I was inclined to attempt it. I began to pray, to read the Scripture, and keep a sort of diary. I was presently religious in my own eyes; but alas!

alas! this seeming goodness had no solid foundation, but passed away like a morning cloud, or the early dew. I was soon weary, gradually gave it up, and became worse than before: Instead of prayer, I learned to curse and blaspheme, and was exceedingly wicked when from under my parents' view. All this was before I was twelve years old. About that time I had a dangerous fall from a horse; I was thrown I believe within a few inches of a hedge-row newly cut down: I got no hurt; but could not avoid taking notice of a gracious providence in my deliverance; for had I fell upon the stakes, I had inevitably been killed. My conscience suggested to me the dreadful consequences, if in such a state I had been summoned to appear before God. I presently broke off from my profane practices, and appeared quite altered; but it was not long before I declined again. These struggles between sin and conscience were often repeated; but the consequence was, that every relapse sunk me still into greater depths of wickedness. I was once rouzed by the loss of an intimate companion. We had agreed to go on board a man of war (I think it was on a *Sunday*);
but

but I providentially came too late; the boat was overset, and he and several others were drowned. I was invited to the funeral of my play-fellow, and was exceedingly affected, to think that by a delay of a few minutes (which had much displeased and angered me, till I saw the event) my life had been preserved. However, this likewise was soon forgot. At another time the perusal of the *Family Instructor* put me upon a partial and transient reformation. In brief, though I cannot distinctly relate particulars, I think I took up and laid aside a religious profession three or four different times before I was sixteen years of age: but all this while my heart was insincere. I often saw a necessity of religion as a means of escaping hell; but I loved sin, and was unwilling to forsake it. Instances of this I can remember were frequent in the midst of all my forms; I was so strangely blind and stupid, that sometimes when I have been determined upon things which I knew were sinful, and contrary to my duty, I could not go on quietly till I had first dispatched my ordinary task of prayer, in which I have grudged every moment of my time; and when this

was

was finished, my conscience was in some measure pacified, and I could rush into folly with little remorse.

My last reform was the most remarkable, both for degree and continuance. Of this period, at least of some part of it, I may say in the Apostle's words, "After "the strictest sect of our religion, I lived "a Pharisee." I did every thing that might be expected from a person intirely ignorant of God's righteousness, and desirous to establish his own. I spent the greatest part of every day in reading the Scriptures, meditation and prayer. I fasted often; I even abstained from all animal food for three months; I would hardly answer a question, for fear of speaking an idle word. I seemed to bemoan my former miscarriages very earnestly, sometimes with tears. In short, I became an ascetic, and endeavoured, so far as my situation would permit, to renounce society, that I might avoid temptation. I continued in this serious mood (I cannot give it a higher title) for more than two years, without any considerable breaking off: but it was a poor religion; it left me, in many respects, under the power of sin, and, so far

as

as it prevailed, only tended to make me gloomy, stupid, unsociable, and useless,

Such was the frame of my mind when I became acquainted with Lord Shaftesbury. I saw the 2d vol. of his *Characteristics*, in a petty shop at Middleburg in Holland. The title allured me to buy it, and the style and manner gave me great pleasure in reading, especially the second piece, which his Lordship with great propriety has intitled a *Rhapsody*. Nothing could be more suited to the romantic turn of my mind, than the address of this pompous declamation; of the design and tendency I was not aware: I thought the author a most religious person, and that I had only to follow him and be happy. Thus, with fine words and fair speeches my simple heart was beguiled. This book was always in my hand: I read it till I could very nearly repeat the Rhapsody *verbatim* from beginning to end. No immediate effect followed, but it operated like a slow poison, and prepared the way for all that followed.

This letter brings my history down to December 1742. I was then lately returned from a voyage, and my father not intending

tending me for the sea again, was thinking how to settle me in the world: but I had little life or spirit for business: I knew but little of men and things. I was fond of a visionary scheme of a contemplative life, a medley of religion, philosophy, and indolence, and was quite averse to the thoughts of an industrious application to business. At length a merchant in Liverpool, an intimate friend of my father's, (to whom, as the instrument of God's goodness, I have since been chiefly indebted for all my earthly comforts), proposed to send me for some years to Jamaica, and to charge himself with the care of my future fortune. I consented to this, and every thing was prepared for my voyage. I was upon the point of setting out the following week. In the mean time my father sent me on some business to a place a few miles beyond Maidstone in Kent; and this little journey, which was to have been only for three or four days, occasioned a sudden and remarkable turn, which roused me from the habitual indolence I had contracted, and gave rise to the series of uncommon dispensations, of which you desire a more particular account. So true it is, that the way

" way of man is not in himself; it is
" not in man that walketh to direct his
" steps."

I am affectionately,

Yours in the best bonds.

January 13. 1763.

LETTER

LETTER III.

Dear Sir,

A Few days before my intended journey into Kent, I received an invitation to visit a family in that county.——They were distant relations, but very intimate friends of my dear mother. She died in their house; but a coolness took place upon my father's second marriage, and I had heard nothing of them for many years. As my road lay within half a mile of their house, I obtained my father's leave to call on them. I was however very indifferent about it, and sometimes thought of passing on: however I went. I was known at first sight before I could tell my name, and met with the kindest reception, as the child of a dear deceased friend. My friends had two daughters——The eldest (as I understood some years afterwards) had been often considered by her mother and mine, as a future wife for me, from the time of her birth. I know indeed that intimate friends frequently amuse themselves with such di-

stant

stant prospects for their children, and that they miscarry much oftner than succeed. I do not say that my mother predicted what was to happen, yet there was something remarkable in the manner of its taking place. All intercourse between the families had been long broken off; I was going into a foreign country, and only called to pay a hasty visit; and this I should not have thought of, but for a message received just at that crisis (for I had not been invited at any time before). Thus the circumstances were precarious in the highest degree, and the event was as extraordinary. Almost at the first sight of this girl (for she was then under fourteen) I was impressed with an affection for her, which never abated or lost its influence a single moment in my heart from that hour. In degree, it actually equalled all that the writers of romance have imagined; in duration, it was unalterable. I soon lost all sense of religion, and became deaf to the remonstrances of conscience and prudence; but my regard for her was always the same; and I may perhaps venture to say, that none of the scenes of misery and wickedness I afterwards experienced, ever banished her a single hour together from my waking thoughts, for the seven following years.

Give me leave, Sir, to reflect a little upon this unexpected incident, and to consider its influence upon my future life, and how far it was subservient to the views of divine Providence concerning me, which seem to have been twofold: that by being given up for a while to the consequences of my own wilfulness, and afterwards reclaimed by a high hand, my case, so far as it should be known, might be both a warning and an encouragement to others.

In the first place, hardly any thing less than this violent and commanding passion, would have been sufficient to awaken me from the dull melancholy habit I had contracted. I was almost a misanthrope, notwithstanding I so much admired the pictures of virtue and benevolence as drawn by Lord Shaftesbury; but now my reluctance to active life was overpowered at once, and I was willing to be or to do any thing which might subserve the accomplishment of my wishes at some future time.

Farther, when I afterwards made shipwreck of faith, hope, and conscience, my love

love to this person was the only remaining principle which in any degree supplied their place; and the bare possibility of seeing her again, was the only present and obvious means of restraining me from the most horrid designs against myself and others.

But then the ill effects it brought upon me counterballanced these advantages. The interval usually stiled the time of courtship, is indeed a pleasing part of life, where there is a mutual affection, the consent of friends, a reasonable prospect as to settlement, and the whole is conducted in a prudential manner, and in subordination to the will and fear of God. When things are thus situated, it is a blessing to be susceptive of the tender passions; but when these concomitants are wanting, what we call *love* is the most tormenting passion in *itself*, and the most destructive in its *consequences*, that can be named. And they were all wanting in my case. I durst not mention it to her friends, or to my own, nor indeed for a considerable time to herself, as I could make no proposals: it remained as a dark fire, locked up in my own breast, which gave me a constant uneasiness

uneasiness. By introducing an idolatrous regard to a creature, it greatly weakened my sense of religion, and made farther way for the entrance of infidel principles; and though it seemed to promise great things, as an incentive to diligence and activity in life, in reality it performed nothing. I often formed mighty projects in my mind of what I would willingly do or suffer for the sake of her I loved; yet while I could have her company, I was incapable of forcing myself away, to improve opportunities that offered. Still less could it do in regulating my manners. It did not prevent me from engaging in a long train of excess and riot, utterly unworthy the honourable pretensions I had formed. And though, through the wonderful interposition of Divine Goodness, the maze of my follies was at length unravelled, and my wishes crowned in such a manner as overpaid my sufferings; yet I am sure I would not go through the same series of trouble again, to possess all the treasures of both the Indies. I have enlarged more than I intended on this point, as perhaps these papers may be useful to caution others against indulging an un-
governable

governable paffion, by my painful experience. How often may such headstrong votaries be said " To sow the wind, and " to reap the whirlwind."

My heart being now fixed and rivetted to a particular object, I considered every thing I was concerned with in a new light. I concluded it would be absolutely impossible to live at such a distance as Jamaica, for a term of four or five years, and therefore determined, at all events, that I would not go. I could not bear either to acquaint my father with the true reason, or to invent a false one; therefore, without taking any notice to him why I did so, I stayed three weeks, instead of three days, in Kent, till I thought (as it proved) the opportunity would be lost, and the ships sailed. I then returned to London. I had highly displeased my father by this disobedience; but he was more easily reconciled than I could have expected. In a little time I sailed with a friend of his to Venice. In this voyage I was exposed to the company and ill example of the common sailors, among whom I ranked. Importunity and opportunity presenting every day, I once more began to relax from the sobriety and

order

order which I had obſerved, in ſome degree, for more than two years—I was ſometimes pierced with ſharp convictions; but though I made a few faint efforts to ſtop, I never recovered from this declenſion, as I had done from ſeveral before: I did not, indeed, as yet turn out profligate; but I was making large ſtrides towards a total apoſtacy from God. The moſt remarkable check and alarm I received (and, for what I know, the laſt) was by a dream, which made a very ſtrong, though not an abiding impreſſion upon my mind.

The conſideration of who I am writing to, renders it needleſs for me either to enter upon a diſcuſſion of the nature of dreams in general, or to make an apology for recording my own. Thoſe who acknowledge Scripture, will allow that there have been monitory and ſupernatural dreams, evident communications from heaven, either directing or foretelling future events: and thoſe who are acquainted with the hiſtory and experience of the people of God, are well aſſured, that ſuch intimations have not been totally withheld in any period down to the preſent times. Reaſon, far from contradicting this

ſuppo-

supposition, strongly pleads for it, where the process of reasoning is rightly understood, and carefully pursued. So that a late eminent writer *, who, I presume, is not generally charged with enthusiasm, undertakes to prove, that the phaenomenon of dreaming is inexplicable at least, if not absolutely impossible, without taking in the agency and intervention of spiritual beings, to us invisible. I would refer the incredulous to him. For my own part, I can say, without scruple, " The dream is " certain, and the interpretation there- " of sure." I am sure I dreamed to 'the following effect; and I cannot doubt, from what I have seen since, that it had a direct and easy application to my own circumstances, to the dangers in which I was about to plunge myself, and to the unmerited deliverance and mercy which God would be pleased to afford me in the time of my distress.

Though I have wrote out a relation of this dream more than once for others, it has happened, that I never reserved a copy; but the principal incidents are so deeply ingraven on my memory, that I believe I

---

* Baxter on the *vis inertiæ*.

am not liable to any confiderable variations in repeating the account. The fcene prefented to my imagination was the harbour of Venice, where we had lately been. I thought it was night, and my watch upon the deck; and that as I was walking to and fro by myfelf, a perfon came to me, (I do not remember from whence), and brought me a ring, with an exprefs charge to keep it carefully; affuring me, that while I preferved that ring, I fhould be happy and fuccefsful; but, if I loft or parted with it, I muft expect nothing but trouble and mifery. I accepted the prefent and the terms willingly, not in the leaft doubting my own care to preferve it, and highly fatisfied to have my happinefs in my own keeping. I was engaged in thefe thoughts, when a fecond perfon came to me, and obferving the ring on my finger, took occafion to afk me fome queftions concerning it. I readily told him its virtues, and his anfwer expreffed a furprize at my weaknefs, in expecting fuch effects from a ring. I think he reafoned with me fome time; upon the impoffibility of the thing, and at length urged me, in direct terms, to throw it away. At firft, I was

D   fhocked

shocked at the proposal, but his insinuations prevailed. I began to reason and doubt myself, and at last plucked it off my finger, and dropped it over the ship's side into the water, which it had no sooner touched, than I saw, the same instant, a terrible fire burst out from a range of the mountains, (a part of the Alps), which appeared at some distance behind the city of Venice. I saw the hills as distinct as if awake, and they were all in flames. I perceived too late my folly; and my tempter, with an air of insult, informed me, that all the mercy God had in reserve for me was comprised in that ring, which I had wilfully thrown away. I understood that I must now go with him to the burning mountains, and that all the flames I saw were kindled upon my account. I trembled, and was in a great agony; so that it was surprising I did not then awake: but my dream continued, and when I thought myself upon the point of a constrained departure, and stood, self-condemned, without plea or hope, suddenly, either a third person, or the same who brought the ring at first, came to me, (I am not certain which), and demanded the

cause

cause of my grief. I told him the plain case, confessing that I had ruined myself wilfully, and deserved no pity. He blamed my rashness, and asked if I should be wiser, supposing I had my ring again? I could hardly answer to this; for I thought it was gone beyond recall. I believe, indeed, I had not time to answer, before I saw this unexpected friend go down under the water, just in the spot where I had dropped it, and he soon returned, bringing the ring with him. The moment he came on board, the flames in the mountains were extinguished, and my seducer left me. Then was " the prey taken from the hand of " the mighty, and the lawful captive de- " livered." My fears were at an end, and with joy and gratitude I approached my kind deliverer to receive the ring again; but he refused to return it, and spoke to this effect: " If you should be intrusted " with this ring again, you would very " soon bring yourself into the same di- " stress; you are not able to keep it; but " I will preserve it for you, and whenever " it is needful, will produce it in your be- " half."——Upon this I awoke, in a state of mind not to be described: I could hardly ly eat or sleep, or transact my necessary business for two or three days; but the impression soon wore off, and in a little time I totally forgot it; and I think it hardly occurred to my mind again, till several years afterwards. It will appear, in the course of these papers, that a time came, when I found myself in circumstances very nearly resembling those suggested by this extraordinary dream, when I stood helpless and hopeless upon the brink of an awful eternity: and I doubt not, but had the eyes of my mind been then opened, I should have seen my grand enemy, who had seduced me, wilfully to renounce and cast away my religious profession, and to involve myself in the most complicated crimes; I say, I should probably have seen him pleased with my agonies, and waiting for a permission to seize and bear away my soul to his place of torment. I should perhaps have seen likewise that JESUS, whom I had persecuted and defied, rebuking the adversary, challenging me for his own, as a brand plucked out of the fire, and saying, " Deliver him from going down into " the pit; I have found a ransom." However, though I saw not these things, I

found

found the benefit; I obtained mercy. The Lord answered for me in the day of my distress; and, blessed be his name, he who restored the ring, (or what was signified by it), vouchsafes to keep it. O what an unspeakable comfort is this, that I am not in mine own keeping! "The Lord is my "shepherd:" I have been enabled to trust my all in his hands, and I know in whom I have believed. Satan still desires to have me, that he might sift me as wheat; but my Saviour has prayed for me, that my faith may not fail. Here is my security and power; a bulwark, against which the gates of hell cannot prevail. But for this, many a time and often (if possible) I should have ruined myself since my first deliverance, nay, I should fall, and stumble, and perish still, after all that the Lord has done for me, if his faithfulness was not engaged in my behalf, to be my sun and shield even unto death.—"Bless the Lord, O my "soul!"

Nothing very remarkable occurred in the following part of that voyage. I returned home December 1743, and soon after repeated my visit to Kent, where I protracted my stay in the same imprudent manner

manner I had done before, which again disappointed my father's designs in my favour, and almost provoked him to disown me. Before any thing suitable offered again, I was impressed, (owing entirely to my own thoughtless conduct, which was all of a piece), and put on board a tender; it was at a critical juncture, when the French fleets were hovering upon our coast, so that my father was incapable to procure my release. In a few days I was sent on board the Harwich man of war at the Nore: I entered here upon quite a new scene of life, and endured much hardship for about a month. My father was then willing that I should remain in the navy, as a war was daily expected, and procured me a recommendation to the Captain, who took me upon the quarter-deck as a midshipman. I had now an easy life as to externals, and might have gained respect; but my mind was unsettled, and my behaviour very indifferent. I here met with companions who completed the ruin of my principles; and though I affected to talk of virtue, and was not so outwardly abandoned as afterwards, yet my delight and habitual practice was wickedness. My chief intimate

mate was a person of exceeding good natural talents, and much observation: he
was the greatest master of what is called *the free-thinking scheme* I remember to
have met with, and knew how to insinu-
ate his sentiments in the most plausible
way—And his zeal was equal to his address; he could hardly have laboured more
in the cause, if he had expected to gain
heaven by it. Allow me to add, while I
think of it, that this man, whom I honoured as my master, and whose practice I a-
dopted so eagerly, perished in the same way
as I expected to have done. I have been
told, that he was overtaken in a voyage
from Lisbon with a violent storm; the
vessel and people escaped, but a great sea
broke on board, and swept him into eternity.——Thus the Lord spares or punishes
according to his sovereign pleasure! But
to return—I was fond of his company, and
having myself a smattering of books, was
eager enough to shew my reading. He
soon perceived my case, that I had not
wholly broke through the restraints of conscience, and therefore did not shock me at
first with too broad intimations of his design; he rather, as I thought, spoke fa-
vourably

vourably of religion; but when he had gained my confidence, he began to speak plainer; and perceiving my ignorant attachment to the *Characteristics*, he joined issue with me upon that book, and convinced me, that I had never understood it. In a word, he so plied me with objections and arguments, that my depraved heart was soon gained, and I entered into his plan with all my spirit. Thus, like an unwary sailor who quits his port just before a rising storm, I renounced the hopes and comforts of the gospel, at the very time when every other comfort was about to fail me.

In December 1744 the Harwich was in the Downs, bound to the East Indies. The Captain gave me liberty to go on shore for a day; but without consulting prudence, or regarding consequences, I took horse, and following the dictates of my restless passion, I went to take a last leave of her I loved. I had little satisfaction in the interview, as I was sensible that I was taking pains to multiply my own troubles. The short time I could stay passed like a dream, and on New-year's day 1745 I took my leave to return to the ship. The Captain was prevailed on to excuse my absence, fence; but this rash step (especially as it was not the first liberty of the kind I had taken) highly displeased him, and lost me his favour, which I never recovered.

At length we sailed from Spithead with a very large fleet. We put into Torbay with a change of wind, but it returning fair again, we sailed the next day. Several of our fleet were lost in attempting to leave that place; but the following night the whole fleet was greatly endangered upon the coast of Cornwall, by a storm from the southward. The darkness of the night, and the number of the vessels, occasioned much confusion and damage. Our ship, though several times in imminent danger of being run down by other vessels, escaped unhurt; but many suffered much, particularly the Admiral. This occasioned our putting back to Plymouth.

While we lay at Plymouth I heard that my father, who had interest in some of the ships lately lost, was come down to Torbay. He had a connection at that time with the African company. I thought if I could get to him, he might easily introduce me into that service, which would be better than pursuing a long uncertain voyage to the East Indies. It was a maxim with me in those unhappy days, *never to deliberate;* the thought hardly occurred to me, but I was resolved to leave the ship at all events: I did so, and in the wrongest manner possible. I was sent one day in the boat, to take care that none of the people deserted, but I betrayed my trust, and went off myself. I knew not what road to take, and durst not ask, for fear of being suspected; yet having some general idea of the country, I guessed right, and when I had travelled some miles, I found, upon enquiry, that I was on the road to Dartmouth. All went smoothly that day, and part of the next; I walked apace, and expected to have been with my father in about two hours, when I was met by a small party of soldiers: I could not avoid or deceive them. They brought me back to Plymouth; I walked through the streets guarded like a felon—My heart was full of indignation, shame, and fear.——I was confined two days in the guardhouse, then sent on board my ship, kept a while in irons, then publicly stripped and whipped, after which I was degraded from my office, and all my former companions forbidden to shew me the least favour, or even to speak to me.——As midshipman I had been entitled

tled to some command, which (being sufficiently haughty and vain) I had not been backward to exert.——I was now in my turn brought down to a level with the lowest, and exposed to the insults of all.

And as my present situation was uncomfortable, my future prospects were still worse; the evils I suffered were likely to grow heavier every day. While my catataſtrophe was recent, the officers, and my quondam brethren, were something disposed to screen me from ill usage; but during the little time I remained with them afterwards I found them cool very fast in their endeavours to protect me. Indeed they could not avoid it, without running a great risk of sharing with me; for the Captain, tho' in general a humane man, who behaved very well to the ship's company, was almost implacable in his resentment when he had been greatly offended, and took several occasions to shew himself so to me, and the voyage was expected to be (as it proved) for five years. Yet I think nothing I either felt or feared distressed me so much as to see myself thus forcibly torn away from the object of my affections, under a great impoſſibility of seeing her again, and a much greater of returning in such a

manner

manner as would give me hopes of seeing her mine. Thus I was as miserable on all hands as could well be imagined. My breast was filled with the most excruciating passions, eager desire, bitter rage, and black despair.—Every hour exposed me to some new insult and hardship, with no hope of relief or mitigation; no friend to take my part, or to listen to my complaint. Whether I looked inward or outward, I could perceive nothing but darkness and misery. I think no case, except that of a conscience wounded by the wrath of God, could be more dreadful than mine: I cannot express with what wishfulness and regret I cast my last looks upon the English shore; I kept my eyes fixed upon it, till the ship's distance increasing, it insensibly disappeared; and when I could see it no longer, I was tempted to throw myself into the sea, which (according to the wicked system I had adopted) would put a period to all my sorrows at once. But the secret hand of God restrained me. Help me to praise him, dear Sir, for his wonderful goodness to the most unworthy of all his creatures.

I am

Your most obliged servant,

January 15. 1763.

LETTER IV.

Dear Sir,

THough I defired your inftructions as to the manner and extent of thefe memoirs, I began to write before I received them, and had almoft finifhed the preceding fheet when your favour of the 11th came to hand. I fhall find another occafion to acknowledge my fenfe of your kind expreffions of friendfhip, which I pray the Lord I may never give you caufe to repent or withdraw: at prefent I fhall confine myfelf to what more particularly relates to the tafk affigned me. I fhall obey you, Sir, in taking notice of the little incidents you recall to my memory, and of others of the like nature, which, without your direction, I fhould have thought too trivial, and too much my own to deferve mentioning. When I began the eight letters, I intended to fay no more of myfelf than might be neceffary to illuftrate the wonders of divine Providence and grace in the leading turns of my life; but I account your judgment a sufficient warrant for enlarging my plan.

Amongst other things, you desired a more explicit account of the state and progress of my courtship, as it is usually phrased. This was the point in which I thought it especially became me to be very brief; but I submit to you; and this seems a proper place to resume it, by telling you how it stood at the time of my leaving England. When my inclinations first discovered themselves, both parties were so young, that no one but myself considered it in a serious view. It served for tea-table talk amongst our friends, and nothing farther was expected from it. But afterwards, when my passion seemed to have abiding effects, so that in an interval of two years it was not at all abated, and especially as it occasioned me to act without any regard to prudence or interest, or my father's designs, and as there was a coolness between him and the family, her parents began to consider it as a matter of consequence; and when I took my last leave of them, her mother, at the same time she expressed the most tender affection for me, as if I had been her own child, told

told me, That though she had no objections to make, upon a supposition that at a maturer age there should be a probability of our engaging upon a prudent prospect; yet as things then stood, she thought herself obliged to interfere; and therefore desired I would no more think of returning to their house (unless her daughter was from home) till such time as I could either prevail with myself entirely to give up my pretensions, or could assure her that I had my father's express consent to go on. Much depended on Mrs N*****'s part in this affair; it was something difficult; but though she was young, gay, and quite unpractised in such matters, she was directed to a happy medium. A positive encouragement, or an absolute refusal, would have been attended with equal, though different disadvantages. But without much studying about it, I found her always upon her guard: she had penetration to see her absolute power over me, and prudence to make a proper use of it; she would neither understand my hints, nor give me room to come to a direct explanation. She has said since, that from the first discovery of my regard, and long before the thought was

agreeable

agreeable to her, she had often an unaccountable impression upon her mind, that sooner or later she should be mine. Upon these terms we parted.

I now return to my voyage. During our passage to Madeira I was a prey to the most gloomy thoughts. Though I had well deserved all I met with, and the Captain might have been justified if he had carried his resentment still farther; yet my pride at that time suggested that I had been grossly injured: and this so far wrought upon my wicked heart, that I actually formed designs against his life; and this was one reason that made me willing to prolong my own. I was sometimes divided between the two, not thinking it practicable to effect both. The Lord had now to appearance given me up to judicial hardness; I was capable of any thing. I had not the least fear of God before my eyes, nor (so far as I remember) the least sensibility of conscience. I was possessed of so strong a spirit of delusion that I believed my own lie, and was firmly persuaded, that after death I should cease to be. —Yet the Lord preserved me!—Some intervals of sober reflection would at times take

take place: when I have chosen death rather than life, a ray of hope would come in, (though there was little probability for such a hope), that I should yet see better days; that I might again return to England, and have my wishes crowned, if I did not wilfully throw myself away. In a word, my love to Mrs N***** was now the only restraint I had left. Though I neither feared God nor regarded men, I could not bear that *she* should think meanly of me when I was dead. As in the outward concerns of life, the weakest means are often employed by divine Providence to produce great effects, beyond their common influence, (as when a disease, for instance, has been removed by a fright), so I found it then; this single thought, which had not restrained me from a thousand smaller evils, proved my only and effectual barrier against the greatest and most fatal temptations. How long I could have supported this conflict, or what, humanly speaking, would have been the consequence of my continuing in that situation, I cannot say; but the Lord, whom I little thought of, knew my danger, and was providing for my deliverance.

Two things I had determined when at Plymouth, that I would *not* go to India, and that I *would* go to Guinea; and such indeed was the Lord's will concerning me; but they were to be accomplished in His way, not in my own. We had been now at Madeira some time; the business of the fleet was compleated, and we were to sail the following day. On that memorable morning I was late in bed, and had slept longer, but that one of the midshipmen (an old companion) came down, and, between jest and earnest, bid me rise; and as I did not immediately comply, he cut down the hammock or bed in which I lay, which forced me to dress myself. I was very angry, but durst not resent it. I was little aware how much his caprice affected me, and that this person, who had no design in what he did, was the messenger of God's providence. I said little, but went upon deck, where I that moment saw a man putting his cloaths into a boat, who told me, he was going to leave us. Upon inquiring, I was informed, that two men from a Guinea ship, which lay near us, had entered on board the Harwich, and that the Commodore,

(the

(the prefent Sir George Pocock), had ordered the Captain to fend two others in their room. My heart inftantly burned like fire.——I begged the boat might be detained a few minutes; I ran to the Lieutenants, and intreated them to intercede with the Captain that I might be difmiffed upon this occafion. Though I had been formerly upon ill terms with thefe officers, and had difobliged them all in their turns, yet they had pitied my cafe, and were ready to ferve me now. The Captain, who when we were at Plymouth had refufed to exchange me, though at the requeft of Admiral Medley, was now eafily prevailed on. I believe, in little more than half an hour from my being afleep in my bed, I faw myfelf difcharged, and fafe on board another fhip. This was one of the many critical turns of my life, in which the Lord was pleafed to difplay his providence and care, by caufing many unexpected circumftances to concur in almoft an inftant of time. Thefe fudden opportunities were feveral times repeated; each of them brought me into an entire new fcene of action, and they were ufually delayed to almoft the laft moment in which they could have taken place.

The ship I went on board was bound to Sierra Leon, and the adjacent parts of what is called *the windward coast of Africa*. The commander, I found, was acquainted with my father; he received me very kindly, and made fair professions of assistance; and I believe he would have been my friend: but without making the least advantage of former mistakes and troubles, pursued the same course; nay, if possible, acted much worse. On board the Harwich, though my principles were totally corrupted, yet, as upon my first going there I was in some degree staid and serious, the remembrance of this made me ashamed of breaking out in that notorious manner I could otherwise have indulged. But now entering amongst strangers, I could appear without disguise; and I well remember, that while I was passing from the one ship to the other, this was one reason why I rejoiced in the exchange, and one reflection I made upon the occasion, *viz.* " That I now might be as abandoned " as I pleased, without any controul;" and from this time I was exceedingly vile indeed, little if any thing short of that animated description of an almost irrecoverable

able state, which we have in 2 *Peter* ii. 14. I not only sinned with a high hand myself, but made it my study to tempt and seduce others upon every occasion; nay, I eagerly sought occasion, sometimes to my own hazard and hurt. One natural consequence of this carriage was, a loss of the favour of my new Captain; not that he was at all religious, or disliked my wickedness any further than it affected his interest, but I became careless and disobedient: I did not please him, because I did not intend it; and as he was a man of an odd temper likewise, we the more easily disagreed. Besides, I had a little of that unlucky wit, which can do little more than multiply troubles and enemies to its possessor; and, upon some imagined affront, I made a song, in which I ridiculed his ship, his designs, and his person, and soon taught it to the whole ship's company. Such was the ungrateful return I made for his offers of friendship and protection. I had mentioned no names, but the allusion was plain, and he was no stranger either to the intention or the author.——I shall say no more of this part of my story; let it be buried in eternal silence.——But let me

not

not be silent from the praise of that grace which could pardon, that blood which could expiate, such sins as mine: Yea, "the E-thiopian may change his skin, and the leopard his spots," since I, who was the willing slave of every evil, possessed with a legion of unclean spirits, have been spared, and saved, and changed, to stand as a monument of his almighty power for ever.

Thus I went on for about six months, by which time the ship was preparing to leave the coast. A few days before she sailed the Captain died. I was not upon much better terms with his mate, who now succeeded to the command, and had, upon some occasion, treated me ill. I made no doubt but if I went with him to the West Indies, he would put me on board a man of war; and this, from what I had known already, was more dreadful to me than death. To avoid it, I determined to remain in Africa, and amused myself with many golden dreams, that here I should find an opportunity of improving my fortune.

There are still upon that part of the coast a few white men settled, (and there were

were many more at the time I was first there), whose business it was to purchase slaves, &c. in the rivers and country adjacent, and sell them to the ships at an advanced price. One of these, who at first landed in my indigent circumstances, had acquired considerable wealth: he had lately been in England, and was returning in the vessel I was in, of which he owned a quarter part. His example impressed me with hopes of the same success; and, upon condition of entering into his service, I obtained my discharge. I had not the precaution to make any terms, but trusted to his generosity. I received no compensation for my time on board the ship, but a bill upon the owners in England, which was never paid, for they failed before my return. The day the vessel sailed, I landed upon the island of Benanoes, with little more than the cloaths upon my back, as if I had escaped shipwreck. I am,

Dear Sir,

Yours, &c.

January 17. 1763.

LETTER

LETTER V.

Dear Sir,

THere seems an important instruction, and of frequent use, in these words of our dear Lord, " Mine hour is not yet " come." The two following years, of which I am now to give some account, will seem as an absolute blank in a very short life: but as the Lord's hour of grace was not yet come, I was to have still deeper experience of the dreadful state of the heart of man when left to itself; I have seen frequent cause since to admire the mercy of the Lord, in banishing me to those distant parts, and almost excluding me from human society, at a time when I was big with mischief, and, like one infected with a pestilence, was capable of spreading a taint where-ever I went. Had my affairs taken a different turn, had I succeeded in my designs, and remained in England, my sad story would probably have been worse. Worse in myself, indeed, I could have hardly been; but my wickedness
would

would have had greater scope; I might have been very hurtful to others, and multiplied irreparable evils. But the Lord wisely placed me where I could do little harm. The few I had to converse with were too much like myself, and I was soon brought into such abject circumstances, that I was too low to have any influence. I was rather shunned and despised than imitated; there being few, even of the negroes themselves, (during the first year of my residence among them), but thought themselves too good to speak to me. I was as yet an " outcast lying in my blood," (*Ezek.* xvi.) and, to all appearance, exposed to perish.——But the Lord beheld me with mercy—he did not strike me to hell, as I justly deserved; " he passed by me " when I was in my blood, and bid me " live." But the appointed time for the manifestation of his love, to cover all my iniquities with the robe of his righteousness, and to admit me to the privileges of his children, was not till long afterwards; yet even now he bid me *live*, and I can only ascribe it to his secret upholding power, that what I suffered in a part of this interval, did not bereave me either of my life or senses; yet, as by these sufferings, the force of my evil examples and inclinations was lessened, I have reason to account them amongst my mercies.

It may not, perhaps, be amiss to digress for a few lines, and give you a very brief sketch of the geography of the circuit I was now confined to, especially as I may have frequent occasion to refer to places I shall now mention; for my trade afterwards, when the Lord gave me to see better days, was chiefly to the same places, and with the same persons, where and by whom I had been considered as upon a level with their meanest slaves. From Cape de Verd, the most western point of Africa, to Cape Mount, the whole coast is full of rivers; the principal are Gambia, Rio Grande, Sierra Leon, and Sherbro. Of the former, as it is well known, and I was never there, I need say nothing. The Rio Grande (like the Nile) divides into many branches near the sea. On the most northerly, called *Cacheo*, the Portuguese have a settlement. The most southern branch, known by the name of *Rio Nuna*, is, or then was, the usual boundary of the white men's trade northward. Sierra Leon is a mountainous

mountainous peninsula, uninhabited, and I believe inacceffible, upon account of the thick woods, excepting thofe parts which ly near the water. The river is large and navigable. From hence, about twelve leagues to the fouth-eaft, are three contiguous iflands, called the *Benanoes*, about twenty miles in circuit: this was about the centre of the white men's refidence. Seven leagues farther, the fame way, ly the Plantanes, three fmall iflands, two miles diftant from the continent at the point, which form one fide of the Sherbro. This river is more properly a *found*, running within a long ifland, and receiving the confluence of feveral large rivers, " *rivers unknown to fong,*" but far more deeply engraven in my remembrance than the Po or Tyber. The fouthermoft of thefe has a very peculiar courfe, almoft parallel to the coaft; fo that in tracing it a great many leagues upwards, it will feldom lead one above three miles, and fometimes not more than half a mile from the fea-fhore. Indeed I know not but that all thefe rivers may have communications with each other, and with the fea in many places, which I have not remarked. If you caft your eyes upon a large map of Africa, while you are reading this, you will have a general idea of the country I was in; for though the maps are very incorrect, most of the places I have mentioned are inserted, and in the same order as I have named them.

My new master had formerly resided near Cape Mount, but now he settled at the Plantanes, upon the largest of the three islands. It is a low sandy island, about two miles in circumference, and almost covered with palm-trees. We immediately began to build a house, and to enter upon trade. I had now some desire to retrieve my lost time, and to exert diligence in what was before me; and he was a man with whom I might have lived tolerably well, if he had not been soon influenced against me: but he was much under the direction of a black woman, who lived with him as a wife. She was a person of some consequence in her own country, and he owed his first rise to her interest. This woman (I know not for what reason) was strangely prejudiced against me from the first; and what made it still worse for me, was a severe fit of illness, which attacked me very soon, before I had opportunity to shew what I could or would

would do in his service. I was sick when he sailed in a shallop to Rio Nuna, and he left me in her hands. At first I was taken some care of, but as I did not recover very soon, she grew weary, and entirely neglected me. I had sometimes not a little difficulty to procure a draught of cold water when burning with a fever. My bed was a mat spread upon a board or chest, and a log of wood my pillow. When my fever left me, and my appetite returned, I would gladly have eaten, but there was no one gave unto me. She lived in plenty herself, but hardly allowed me sufficient to sustain life, except now and then, when in the highest good humour, she would send me victuals in her own plate after she had dined; and this (so greatly was my pride humbled) I received with thanks and eagerness, as the most needy beggar does an alms. Once, I well remember, I was called to receive this bounty from her own hand, but being exceedingly weak and feeble, I dropped the plate. Those who live in plenty can hardly conceive how this loss touched me; but she had the cruelty to laugh at my disappointment; and tho' the table was covered with dishes, (for she lived much in the European manner), she refused to give me any more. My distress has been at times so great, as to compel me to go by night, and pull up roots in the plantation, (though at the risk of being punished as a thief), which I have eaten raw upon the spot, for fear of discovery. The roots I speak of are very wholesome food, when boiled or roasted, but as unfit to be eaten raw in any quantity as a potatoe. The consequence of this diet, which, after the first experiment, I always expected, and seldom missed, was the same as if I had taken *tartar emetic;* so that I have often returned as empty as I went; yet necessity urged me to repeat the trial several times. I have sometimes been relieved by strangers, nay even by the slaves in the chain, who have secretly brought me victuals, (for they durst not be seen to do it), from their own slender pittance. Next to pressing want, nothing sits harder upon the mind than *scorn* and *contempt;* and of this likewise I had an abundant measure. When I was very slowly recovering, this woman would sometimes pay me a visit, not to pity or relieve, but to insult me. She would call me worthless and indolent,

and

and compel me to walk, which, when I could hardly do, she would set her attendants to mimic my motion, to clap their hands, laugh, throw limes at me; or, if they chose to throw stones, (as I think was the case once or twice), they were not rebuked: but in general, though all who depended on her favour must join in her treatment, yet, when she was out of sight, I was rather pitied than scorned by the meanest of her slaves. At length my master returned from his voyage; I complained of ill usage, but he could not believe me; and as I did it in her hearing, I fared no better for it. But in his second voyage he took me with him. We did pretty well for a while, till a brother-trader he met in the river persuaded him that I was unfaithful, and stole his goods in the night, or when he was on shore. This was almost the only vice I could not be justly charged with: the only remains of a good education I could boast of was, what is commonly called *honesty*; and as far as he had intrusted me, I had been always true; and though my great distress might, in some measure, have excused it, I never once thought of defrauding him in the
smallest

smallest matter. However, the charge was believed, and I condemned without evidence. From that time *he* likewise used me very hardly: whenever he left the vessel, I was locked upon deck, with a pint of rice for my day's allowance; and if he staid longer, I had no relief till his return. Indeed I believe I should have been nearly starved, but for an opportunity of catching fish sometimes. When fowls were killed for his own use, I seldom was allowed any part but the intrails to bait my hooks with: and at what we call *slack water*, that is, about the changing of the tides, when the current was still, I used generally to fish, (for at other times it was not practicable), and I very often succeeded. If I saw a fish upon my hook, my joy was little less than any other person may have found in the accomplishment of the scheme he had most at heart. Such a fish, hastily broiled, or rather half burnt, without sauce, salt, or bread, has afforded me a delicious meal. If I caught none, I might (if I could) sleep away my hunger till the next return of slack water, and then try again. Nor did I suffer less from the inclemency of the weather and the want of cloaths.

The

The rainy season was now advancing; my whole suit was a shirt, a pair of trowsers, a cotton handkerchief instead of a cap, and a cotton cloth, about two yards long, to supply the want of upper garments; and thus accoutred I have been exposed for twenty, thirty, perhaps near forty hours together, in incessant rains, accompanied with strong gales of wind, without the least shelter, when my master was on shore. I feel to this day some faint returns of the violent pains I then contracted. The excessive cold and wet I endured in that voyage, and so soon after I had recovered from a long sickness, quite broke my constitution and my spirits; the latter were soon restored, but the effects of the former still remain with me, as a needful *memento* of the service and wages of sin.

In about two months we returned, and then the rest of the time I remained with him was chiefly spent at the Plantanes, under the same regimen as I have already mentioned. My haughty heart was now brought down, not to a wholesome repentance, not to the language of the prodigal; this was far from me; but my spirits were sunk; I lost all resolution, and almost

most all reflection. I had lost the fierceness which fired me when on board the Harwich, and which made me capable of the most desperate attempts; but I was no further changed than a tyger tamed by hunger—remove the occasion, and he will be as wild as ever.

One thing, though strange, is most true. Though destitute of food and cloathing, depressed to a degree beyond common wretchedness, I could sometimes collect my mind to mathematical studies. I had bought *Barrow*'s *Euclid* at Plymouth; it was the only volume I brought on shore; it was always with me, and I used to take it to remote corners of the island by the sea-side, and draw my *diagrams* with a long stick upon the sand. Thus I often beguiled my sorrows, and almost forgot my feeling—and thus, without any other assistance, I made myself in a good measure master of the first six books of *Euclid*.

I am

Yours, as before.

January 17. 1763.

LETTER

LETTER VI.

Dear Sir,

THere is much piety and spirit in the grateful acknowledgment of Jacob, " With my staff I passed this Jordan, and " now I am become two bands." They are words which ought to affect me with a peculiar emotion. I remember that some of those mournful days, to which my last letter refers, I was busied in planting some *lime* or *lemon trees*. The plants I put in the ground were no longer than a young gooseberry bush: my master and his mistress passing by the place, stopped a while to look at me; at last, " Who knows," says he, " who knows but by the time these trees " grow up and bear, you may go home to " England, obtain the command of a ship, " and return to reap the fruit of your la- " bours; we see strange things sometimes " happen." This, as he intended it, was a cutting sarcasm. I believe he thought it full as probable that I should live to be king of Poland; yet it proved a prediction;

and

and they (one of them at least) lived to see me return from England, in the capacity he had mentioned, and pluck some of the first limes from those very trees. How can I proceed in my relation till I raise a monument to the divine goodness, by comparing the circumstances in which the Lord has since placed me, with what I was at that time! Had you seen me, Sir, then go so pensive and solitary, in the dead of night, to wash my one shirt upon the rocks, and afterwards put it on wet, that it might dry upon my back while I slept; had you seen me so poor a figure, that when a ship's boat came to the island, shame often constrained me to hide myself in the woods from the sight of strangers; especially had you known that my conduct, principles, and heart, were still darker than my outward condition——how little would you have imagined that one, who so fully answered to the συγητοι & μισουντες * of the apostle, was reserved to be so peculiar an instance of the providential care, and exuberant goodness of God. There was at that time but one earnest desire in my heart, which was not contrary and shock-

* Hateful, and hating one another.

ing,

ing, both to religion and reason; that one desire, though my vile licentious life rendered me peculiarly unworthy of success, and though a thousand difficulties seemed to render it impossible, the Lord was pleased to gratify. But this favour, tho' great, and greatly prized, was a small thing compared to the blessings of his grace: he spared me to give me " the knowledge of " himself in the person of Jesus Christ;" in love to my soul, he delivered me from the pit of corruption, and cast all my aggravated sins behind his back. He brought my feet into the paths of peace.——This is indeed the chief article, but it is not the whole. When he made me acceptable to himself in the Beloved, he gave me favour in the sight of others. He raised me new friends, protected and guided me through a long series of dangers, and crowned every day with repeated mercies. To him I owe it that I am still alive, and that I am not still living in hunger, and in thirst, and in nakedness, and the want of all things: into that state I brought myself, but it was He delivered me. He has given me an easy situation in life, some experimental knowledge of his gospel, a large

G acquaint-

acquaintance amongst his people, a friendship and correspondence with several of his most honoured servants.——But it is as difficult to enumerate my present advantages, as it is fully to describe the evils and miseries of the preceding contrast.

I know not exactly how long things continued with me thus, but I believe near a twelvemonth. In this interval I wrote two or three times to my father; I gave him an account of my condition, and desired his assistance; intimating, at the same time, that I had resolved not to return to England, unless he was pleased to send for me. I have likewise letters wrote by me to Mrs N**** in that dismal period; so that at the lowest ebb it seems I still retained a hope of seeing her again. My father applied to his friend in Liverpoole, of whom I have spoken before, who gave orders accordingly to a Captain of his, who was then fitting out for Gambia and Sierra Leon.

Some time within the year, as I have said, I obtained my master's consent to live with another trader, who dwelt upon the same island. Without his consent I could not be taken, and he was unwilling to do it sooner, but it was then brought about.

This

This was an alteration much to my advantage; I was soon decently clothed, lived in plenty, was considered as a companion, and trusted with the care of all his domestic effects, which were to the amount of some thousand pounds. This man had several factories, and white servants in different places, particularly one in Kittam, the river I spoke of, which runs so near along the sea-coast. I was soon appointed to go there, where I had a share in the management of business jointly with another of his servants. We lived as we pleased, business flourished, and our employer was satisfied. Here I began to be wretch enough to think myself *happy*. There is a significant phrase frequently used in those parts, That such a white man is grown *black*. It does not intend an alteration of complexion, but disposition. I have known several who, settling in Africa after the age of thirty or forty, have, at that time of life, been gradually assimilated to the tempers, customs, and ceremonies of the natives, so far as to prefer that country to England; they have even become dupes to all the pretended charms, necromancies, amulets, and divinations of the blinded negroes

negroes, and put more truſt in ſuch things than the wiſer ſort among the natives. A part of this ſpirit of infatuation was growing upon me, (in time perhaps I might have yielded to the whole); I entered into cloſer engagements with the inhabitants, and ſhould have lived and died a wretch amongſt them, if the Lord had not watched over me for good. Not that I had loſt thoſe ideas which chiefly engaged my heart to England, but deſpair of ſeeing them accompliſhed made me willing to remain where I was. I thought I could more eaſily bear the diſappointment in this ſituation than nearer home. But ſo ſoon as I had fixed my connections and plans with theſe views, the Lord providentially interpoſed to break them in pieces, and ſave me from ruin in ſpite of myſelf.

In the mean time, the ſhip that had orders to bring me home arrived at Sierra Leon: the Captain made inquiry for me there, and at the Benanoes; but underſtanding that I was at a great diſtance in the country, he thought no more about me. Without doubt the hand of God directed my being placed at Kittam juſt at this time; for as the ſhip came no nearer than

than the Benanoes, and ſtaid but a few days, if I had been at the Plantanes I could not perhaps have heard of her till ſhe had been failed. The ſame muſt have certainly been the event, had I been ſent to any other factory, of which my new maſter had ſeveral upon different rivers. But though the place I was at was a long way up a river, much more than a hundred miles diſtance from the Plantanes, yet by the peculiar ſituation which I have already noticed, I was ſtill within a mile of the ſeacoaſt. To make the interpoſition more remarkable, I was at that very juncture going in queſt of trade, to a place at ſome diſtance directly from the ſea, and ſhould have ſet out a day or two before, but that we waited for a few articles from the next ſhip that offered, to complete the aſſortment of goods I was to take with me. We uſed ſometimes to walk on the beach, in expectation of ſeeing a veſſel paſs by; but this was very precarious, as at that time the place was not at all reſorted to by ſhips for trade. Many paſſed in the night, others kept at a conſiderable diſtance from the ſhore. In a word, I do not know that any one had ſtopped while I was there, though

some

some had before, upon observing a signal made from the shore. In February 1747, (I know not the exact day), my fellow-servant walking down to the beach in the forenoon, saw a vessel sailing past, and made a smoke in token of trade. She was already a little beyond the place, and as the wind was fair, the Captain was in some demur whether to stop or not; however, had my companion been half an hour later, she would have been gone beyond recall; but he soon saw her come to an anchor, and went on board in a canoe; and this proved the very ship I have spoken of. One of the first questions he was asked was concerning me, and when the Captain understood I was so near, he came on shore to deliver his message. Had an invitation from home reached me when I was sick and starving at the Plantanes, I should have received it as life from the dead; but now, for the reasons already given, I heard it at first with indifference. The Captain, unwilling to lose me, told a story altogether of his own framing; he gave me a very plausible account how he had missed a large packet of letters and papers which he should have brought with him; but this,

he

he said, he was sure of, having had it from my father's own mouth, as well as from his employer, that a person lately dead had left me 400 *l. per annum;* adding further, that if I was any way embarrassed in my circumstances, he had express orders to redeem me, though it should cost one half of his cargo. Every particular of this was false; nor could I myself believe what he said about the estate; but as I had some expectations from an aged relation, I thought a part of it might be true. But I was not long in suspence; for though my father's care and desire to see me had too little weight with me, and would have been insufficient to make me quit my retreat, yet the remembrance of Mrs N****, the hopes of seeing her, and the possibility that accepting this offer might once more put me in a way of gaining her hand, prevailed over all other considerations. The Captain further promised, (and in this he kept his word), that I should lodge in his cabbin, dine at his table, and be his constant companion, without expecting any service from me. And thus I was suddenly freed from a captivity of about fifteen months. I had neither a thought nor a desire of this

change

change one hour before it took place. I embarked with him, and in a few hours loſt ſight of Kittam.

How much is their blindneſs to be pitied who can ſee nothing but chance in events of this ſort! ſo blind and ſtupid was I at that time: I made no reflection, I ſought no direction in what had happened: like a wave of the ſea driven with the wind, and toſſed, I was governed by preſent appearances, and looked no farther. But He, who is eyes to the blind, was leading me in a way that I knew not.

Now I am in ſome meaſure enlightened, I can eaſily perceive, that it is in the adjuſtment and concurrence of theſe ſeemingly fortuitous circumſtances, that the ruling power and wiſdom of God is moſt evidently diſplayed in human affairs. How many ſuch caſual events may we remark in the hiſtory of Joſeph, which had each a neceſſary influence on his enſuing promotion! If he had not dreamed, or if he had not told his dream;—if the Midianites had paſſed by a day ſooner, or a day later; if they had ſold him to any perſon but Potiphar; if his miſtreſs had been a better woman; if Pharaoh's officers had not diſ-

pleaſed

pleased their lord; or if any, or all these things had fell out in any other manner or time than they did, all that followed had been prevented; the promises and purposes of God concerning Israel, their bondage, deliverance, polity, and settlement, must have failed: and as all these things tended to and centered in CHRIST, the promised Saviour, the desire of all nations would not have appeared. Mankind had been still in their sins, without hope, and the counsels of God's eternal love, in favour of sinners, defeated. Thus we may see a connection between Joseph's first dream and the death of our LORD CHRIST, with all its glorious consequences. So strong, though secret, is the concatenation between the *greatest* and the *smallest* events. What a comfortable thought is this to a believer, to know, that amidst all the various interfering designs of men, the Lord has one constant design, which he cannot, will not miss, namely, his own glory in the compleat salvation of his people; and that he is wise, and strong, and faithful, to make even those things which seem contrary to this design, subservient to promote it. You have allowed me to comment upon my own text, yet the length of this observation may need some apology. Believe me to be, with great respect,

Dear Sir,

Your affectionate and obliged servant.

January 18. 1763.

LETTER VII.

Dear Sir,

THE ship I was now on board, as a passenger, was on a trading voyage for gold, ivory, dyers-wood, and bees wax. It requires much longer time to collect a cargo of this sort, than of slaves. The Captain began his trade at Gambia, had been already four or five months in Africa, and continued there a year, or thereabouts, after I was with him; in which time we ranged the whole coast as far as Cape Lopez, which lyes about a degree south of the Equinoctial, and more than a thousand miles farther from England than the place where I embarked. I have little to offer worthy your notice in the course of this tedious voyage. I had no business to employ my thoughts, but sometimes amused myself with mathematics: excepting this, my whole life, when awake, was a course of most horrid impiety and profaneness. I know not that I have ever since met so daring a blasphemer: not

content

content with common oaths and imprecations, I daily invented new ones; so that I was often seriously reproved by the Captain, who was himself a very passionate man, and not at all circumspect in his expressions. From the relation I at times made him of my past adventures, and what he saw of my conduct, and especially towards the close of the voyage, when we met with many disasters, he would often tell me, that, to his great grief, he had a Jonah on board; that a curse attended me where-ever I went; and that all the troubles he met with in the voyage, were owing to his having taken me into the vessel. I shall omit any further particulars, and after mentioning an instance or two of the Lord's mercy to me, while I was thus defying his power and patience, I shall proceed to something more worthy your perusal.

Although I lived long in the excess of almost every other extravagance, I never was fond of drinking; and my father has often been heard to say, that while I avoided drunkenness, he should still entertain hopes of my recovery. But sometimes I would promote a drinking-bout, for a frolic sake, as I termed it; for though I did

not

not love the liquor, I was sold to do iniquity, and delighted in mischief. The last abominable frolic of this sort I engaged in was in the river Gabon; the proposal and expence were my own. Four or five of us one evening sat down upon deck, to see who could hold out longest in drinking geneva and rum alternately: a large sea-shell supplied the place of a glass. I was very unfit for a challenge of this sort; for my head was always incapable of bearing much strong drink. However I began, and proposed the first toast, which I well remember was some imprecation against the person who should *start* first.—This proved to be myself—My brain was soon fired—I arose, and danced about the deck like a madman; and while I was thus diverting my companions, my hat went overboard. By the light of the moon I saw the ship's boat, and eagerly threw myself over the side to get into her, that I might recover my hat. My sight in that circumstance deceived me; for the boat was not within my reach, as I thought, but perhaps twenty feet from the ship's side. I was, however, half overboard, and should in one moment more have plunged myself into the water, when somebody catched hold of my cloaths behind, and pulled me back. This was an amazing escape; for I could not swim if I had been sober; the tide ran very strong; my companions were too much intoxicated to save me; and the rest of the ship's company were asleep. So near was I to appearance of perishing in that dreadful condition, and sinking into eternity under the weight of my own curse.

Another time, at Cape Lopez, some of us had been in the woods, and shot a buffalo, or wild cow: we brought a part of it on board, and carefully marked the place (as I thought) where we left the remainder. In the evening we returned to fetch it, but we set out too late. I undertook to be the guide, but night coming on before we could reach the place, we lost our way.—Sometimes we were in swamps, up to the middle in water, and when we recovered dry land, we could not tell whether we were walking towards the ship, or wandering farther from her.—Every step increased our uncertainty.—The night grew darker, and we were entangled in inextricable woods, where perhaps the foot of man had never trod before him. That part of the
country

country is entirely abandoned to wild beasts, with which it prodigiously abounds. We were indeed in a terrible case, having neither light, food, or arms, and expecting a tyger to rush from behind every tree. The stars were clouded, and we had no compass, to form a judgment which way we were going. Had things continued thus, we had probably perished; but it pleased God, no beast came near us; and after some hours perplexity, the moon arose, and pointed out the eastern quarter. It appeared then, as we had expected, that instead of drawing nearer to the sea-side, we had been penetrating into the country; but by the guidance of the moon we at length came to the water-side, a considerable distance from the ship. We got safe on board, without any other inconvenience than what we suffered from fear and fatigue.

Those, and many other deliverances, were all at that time entirely lost upon me. The admonitions of conscience, which, from successive repulses, had grown weaker and weaker, at length entirely ceased; and for a space of many months, if not for some years, I cannot recollect that I had a single check of that sort. At times I have been visited with sickness, and have believed myself near to death; but I had not the least concern about the consequences. In a word, I seemed to have every mark of final impenitence and rejection; neither judgments nor mercies made the least impression on me.

At length, our business finished, we left Cape Lopez, and, after a few days stay at the island of Annabona, to lay in provisions, we sailed homewards, about the beginning of January 1748. From Annabona to England, without touching at any intermediate port, is a very long navigation, perhaps more than seven thousand miles, if we include the circuit necessary to be made on account of the tradewinds. We sailed first westward, till near the coast of Brazil, then northwards, to the banks of Newfoundland, with the usual variations of wind and weather, and without meeting any thing extraordinary. On these banks we stopped half a day to fish for cod: this was then chiefly for diversion; we had provisions enough, and little expected those fish (as it afterwards proved) would be all we should have to subsist on. We left the
banks

banks March 1, with a hard gale of wind westerly, which pushed us fast homewards. I should here observe, that with the length of this voyage in a hot climate, the vessel was greatly out of repair, and very unfit to support stormy weather; the sails and cordage were likewise very much worn out, and many such circumstances concurred, to render what followed more dangerous. I think it was on the 9th of March, the day before our catastrophe, that I felt a thought pass through my mind, which I had long been a stranger to. Among the few books we had on board, one was Stanhope's *Thomas à Kempis*: I carelessly took it up, as I had often done before, to pass away the time; but I had still read it with the same indifference, as if it was entirely a romance. However, while I was reading this time, an involuntary suggestion arose in my mind, What if these things should be true? I could not bear the force of the inference, as it related to myself, and therefore shut the book presently. My conscience witnessed against me once more, and I concluded, that true or false, I must abide the consequences of my own choice. I put an abrupt end to these reflections, by joining in with some vain conversation or other that came in the way.

But now *the Lord's time was come*, and the conviction I was so unwilling to receive was deeply impressed upon me, by an awful dispensation. I went to bed that night in my usual security and indifference, but was awaked from a sound sleep by the force of a violent sea, which broke on board us. So much of it came down below as filled the cabin I lay in with water. This alarm was followed by a cry from the deck, that the ship was going down, (or sinking.) As soon as I could recover myself, I essayed to go upon deck, but was met upon the ladder by the Captain, who desired me to bring a knife with me. While I returned for the knife, another person went up in my room, who was instantly washed overboard. We had no leisure to lament him; nor did we expect to survive him long; for we soon found the ship was filling with water very fast. The sea had torn away the upper timbers on one side, and made the ship a mere wreck in a few minutes. I shall not affect to describe this disaster in the marine dialect, which would be understood by few; and therefore I can give you but a very inade-

quate

quate idea of it. Taken in all circumstances, it was astonishing, and almost miraculous, that any of us survived to relate the story. We had immediate recourse to the pumps, but the water increased against all our efforts: some of us were set to *bailing* in another part of the vessel, that is, to lade it out with buckets and pails. We had but eleven or twelve people to sustain this service; and notwithstanding all we could do, she was full, or very near it; and then with a common cargo she must have sunk of course: but we had a great quantity of bees-wax and wood on board, which were specifically lighter than the water; and as it pleased God that we received this shock in the very crisis of the gale, towards morning we were enabled to employ some means for our safety, which succeeded beyond hope. In about an hour's time the day began to break, and the wind abated. We expended most of our cloaths and bedding to stop the leaks, (though the weather was exceeding cold, especially to us, who had so lately left a hot climate); over these we nailed pieces of boards, and at last perceived the water abate. At the beginning of this hurry I was little affected;

ed; I pumped hard, and endeavoured to animate myself and my companions: I told one of them, that in a few days this diſtreſs would ſerve us to talk of over a glaſs of wine: but he being a leſs hardened ſinner than myſelf, replied with tears, " No, it is too late now." About nine o'clock, being almoſt ſpent with cold and labour, I went to ſpeak with the Captain, who was buſied elſewhere; and juſt as I was returning from him, I ſaid, almoſt without any meaning, " If this will not do, the " Lord have mercy on us." This, (though ſpoken with little reflection) was the firſt deſire I had breathed for mercy for the ſpace of many years. I was inſtantly ſtruck with my own words, and as Jehu ſaid once, *What haſt thou to do with peace?* ſo it directly occurred, *What mercy can there be for me?* I was obliged to return to the pump, and there I continued till noon, almoſt every paſſing wave breaking over my head; but we made ourſelves faſt with ropes, that we might not be waſhed away. Indeed I expected, that every time the veſſel deſcended in the ſea, ſhe would riſe no more; and though I dreaded death now, and my heart foreboded the worſt, if

the

the scriptures, which I had long since opposed, were indeed true; yet still I was but half convinced, and remained for a space of time in a sullen frame, a mixture of despair and impatience. I thought, if the Christian religion was true I could not be forgiven; and was therefore expecting, and almost, at times, wishing to know the worst of it.

I am,

Sir,

Yours.

January 19. 1763.

LETTER

LETTER VIII.

Dear Sir,

THE 10th (that is in the present style the 21st) of March, is a day much to be remembered by me, and I have never suffered it to pass wholly unnoticed since the year 1748. On that day the Lord sent from on high, and delivered me out of deep waters.—I continued at the pump from *three* in the *morning* till near *noon*, and then I could do no more. I went and lay down upon my bed, uncertain, and almost indifferent, whether I should rise again. In an hour's time I was called, and not being able to pump, I went to the helm, and steered the ship till midnight, excepting a small interval for refreshment. I had here leisure and convenient opportunity for reflection. I began to think of my former religious professions, the extraordinary turns in my life; the calls, warnings, and deliverances I had met with, the licentious course of my conversation, particularly my unparallelled effrontery in making the gospel

spel history (which I could not now be sure was false, though I was not as yet assured it was true) the constant subject of profane ridicule. I thought, allowing the scripture premisses, there never was nor could be such a sinner as myself; and then comparing the advantages I had broken through, I concluded at first that my sins were too great to be forgiven. The scripture likewise seemed to say the same; for I had formerly been well acquainted with the Bible, and many passages upon this occasion returned upon my memory, particularly those awful passages, *Prov.* i. 24.—31. *Heb.* vi. 4. 6. and 2 *Pet.* ii. 20. which seemed so exactly to suit my case and character, as to bring with them a presumptive proof of a divine original. Thus, as I have said, I waited with fear and impatience to receive my inevitable doom. Yet though I had thoughts of this kind, they were exceeding faint and disproportionate; it was not till long after (perhaps several years) till I had gained some clear views of the infinite righteousness and grace of Christ Jesus my Lord, that I had a deep and strong apprehension of my state by nature and practice; and perhaps till then

then I could not have borne the fight. So wonderfully does the Lord proportion the difcoveries of fin and grace, for he knows our frame, and that if he was to put forth the greatnefs of his power, a poor finner would be inftantly overwhelmed, and crufh-ed as a moth. But to return: when I faw, beyond all probability, there was ftill hope of refpite, and heard about fix in the evening, that the fhip was freed from water— there arofe a gleam of hope. I thought I faw the hand of God difplayed in our favour; I began to pray—I could not utter the prayer of faith; I could not draw near to a reconciled God, and call him father. My prayer was like the cry of the ravens, which yet the Lord does not difdain to hear. I now began to think of that JESUS whom I had fo often derided; I recollected the particulars of his life, and of his death; a death for fins not his *own*, but, as I remembered, for the fake of thofe who in their diftrefs fhould put their truft in him. And now I chiefly wanted evidence.———The comfortlefs principles of infidelity were deeply rivetted, and I rather wifhed than believed thefe things were real facts. You will pleafe to obferve, Sir, that I collect the

the strain of the reasonings and exercises of my mind in one view, but I do not say that all this passed at one time. The great question now was, how to obtain *faith?* I speak not of an appropriating faith, (of which I then knew neither the nature nor necessity), but how I should gain an assurance that the scriptures were of divine inspiration, and a sufficient warrant for the exercise of trust and hope in God. One of the first helps I received (in consequence of a determination to examine the New Testament more carefully) was from *Luke* xi. 13. I had been sensible, that to profess faith in Jesus Christ, when in reality I did not believe his history, was no better than a mockery of the heart-searching God; but here I found a Spirit spoken of, which was to be communicated to those who ask it. Upon this I reasoned thus—If this book is true, the promise in this passage must be true likewise: I have need of that very Spirit, by which the whole was wrote, in order to understand it aright. He has engaged here to give that Spirit to those who ask.——I must therefore pray for it, and if it is of God, he will make good his own word. My purposes were strengthened by

John

John vii. 17. I concluded from thence, that though I could not say from my heart that I believed the gospel, yet I would for the present take it for granted, and that by studying it in this light I should be more and more confirmed in it. If what I am writing could be perused by our modern infidels, they would say, (for I too well know their manner), that I was very desirous to persuade myself into this opinion. I confess I was; and so would they be, if the Lord should shew them, as he was pleased to shew me at that time, the absolute necessity of some expedient to interpose between a righteous God and a sinful soul. Upon the gospel scheme I saw at least a peradventure of hope, but on every other side I was surrounded with black unfathomable despair.

The wind was now moderate, but continued fair, and we were still drawing nearer to our port. We began to recover from our consternation, though we were greatly alarmed by our circumstances. We found that the water having floated all our moveables in the hold, all the casks of provision had been beaten to pieces by the violent motion of the ship: on the other hand, live stock, such as pigs, sheep, and poultry, had been washed overboard in the storm. In effect, all the provisions we saved, except the fish I mentioned, and some food of the pulse kind, which used to be given to the hogs, (and there was but little of this left), all our other provisions would have subsisted us but a week at scanty allowance. The sails too were mostly blown away, so that we advanced but slowly even while the wind was fair. We imagined ourselves about a hundred leagues from the land, but were in reality much farther. Thus we proceeded with an alternate prevalence of hopes and fears.——My leisure time was chiefly employed in reading and meditating on the scripture, and praying to the Lord for mercy and instruction.

Things continued thus for four or five days, or perhaps longer, till we were awakened one morning by the joyful shouts of the watch upon deck proclaiming the sight of land. We were all soon raised at the sound. The dawning was uncommonly beautiful, and the light (just strong enough to discover distant objects) presented us with a gladening prospect: it seemed a mountainous coast, about twenty miles from us, terminating in a cape or point, and a little further two or three small islands, or hummocks, as just rising out of the water; the appearance and position seemed exactly answerable to our hopes, resembling the north-west extremity of Ireland, which we were steering for. We sincerely congratulated each other, making no doubt but that, if the wind continued, we should be in safety and plenty the next day. The small remainder of our brandy (which was reduced to little more than a pint) was, by the Captain's orders, distributed amongst us; he added at the same time, "We shall soon have brandy enough." ———We likewise ate up the residue of our bread for joy of this welcome sight, and were in the condition of men suddenly reprieved from death. While we were thus alert, the mate, with a graver tone than the rest, sunk our spirits, by saying, that " he wished it might prove land at last." If one of the common sailors had first said so, I know not but the rest would have beat him for raising such an unreasonable doubt. It brought on however warm debates and disputes whether it was land or no; but the case was soon unanswerably decided,

for

for the day was advancing fast, and in a little time one of our fancied islands began to grow red from the approach of the sun, which soon arose just under it. In a word, we had been prodigal of our bread and brandy too hastily; our land was literally *in nubibus*, nothing but clouds, and in half an hour more the whole appearance was dissipated.——Seamen have often known deceptions of this sort, but in our extremity we were very loth to be undeceived. However, we comforted ourselves, that tho' we could not see the land yet, we should soon, the wind hitherto continuing fair; but alas! we were deprived of this hope likewise.—That very day our fair wind subsided into a calm, and the next morning the gales sprung up from the south-east, directly against us, and continued so for more than a fortnight afterwards. The ship was so wrecked, that we were obliged to keep the wind always on the broken side, unless the weather was quite moderate: thus we were driven, by the wind fixing in that quarter, still further from our port, to the northward of all Ireland, as far as the Lewis or western islands of Scotland, but a long way to the westward.

In a word, our station was such as deprived us of any hope of being relieved by other vessels: it may indeed be questioned, whether our ship was not the very first that had been in that part of the ocean at the same season of the year.

Provisions now began to grow very short; the half of a salted cod was a day's subsistance for twelve people; we had plenty of fresh water, but not a drop of stronger liquor; no bread, hardly any cloaths, and very cold weather. We had incessant labour with the pumps to keep the ship above water. Much labour and little food wasted us fast, and one man died under the hardship. Yet our sufferings were light in comparison of our just fears; we could not afford this bare allowance much longer, but had a terrible prospect of being either starved to death, or reduced to feed upon one another. Our expectations grew darker every day, and I had a further trouble peculiar to myself. The Captain, whose temper was quite soured by distress, was hourly reproaching me (as I formerly observed) as the sole cause of the calamity, and was confident, that if I was thrown overboard, (and not otherwise), they should be preserved

served from death. He did not intend to make the experiment, but the continual repetition of this in my ears gave me much uneasiness, especially as my conscience seconded his words; I thought it very probable that all that had befallen us was on my account. I was at last found out by the powerful hand of God, and condemned in my own breast. However, proceeding in the method I have described, I began to conceive hopes greater than all my fears; especially when at the time we were ready to give up all for lost, and despair was taking place in every countenance, I saw the wind come about to the very point we wished it, so as best to suit that broken part of the ship which must be kept out of the water, and to blow so gentle as our few remaining sails could bear; and thus it continued without any observable alteration or increase, though at an unsettled time of the year, till we once more were called up to see the land, and were convinced that it was land indeed. We saw the island Tory, and the next day anchored in Lough Swilly in Ireland. This was the 8th of April, just four weeks after the damage we sustained from the sea.

When

When we came into this port, our very laſt victuals was boiling in the pot; and before we had been there two hours, the wind, which ſeemed to have been providentially reſtrained till we were in a place of ſafety, began to blow with great violence, ſo that if we had continued at ſea that night in our ſhattered enfeebled condition, we muſt in all human appearance have gone to the bottom. About this time I began to know that there is a God that hears and anſwers prayer. How many times has he appeared for me ſince this great deliverance.—Yet, alas! how diſtruſtful and ungrateful is my heart unto this hour. I am,

  Dear Sir,

   Your obliged humble ſervant.

January 19. 1763.

LETTER

LETTER IX.

Dear Sir,

I Have brought my history down to the time of my arrival in Ireland, 1748; but before I proceed, I would look back a little, to give you some further account of the state of my mind, and how far I was helped against inward difficulties, which beset me at the time I had many outward hardships to struggle with. The straits of hunger, cold, weariness, and the fears of sinking, and starving, I shared in common with others; but, besides these, I felt a heart-bitterness, which was properly my own; no one on board but myself being impressed with any sense of the hand of God in our danger and deliverance, at least not awakened to any concern for their souls. No temporal dispensations can reach the heart, unless the Lord himself applies them. My companions in danger were either quite unaffected, or soon forgot it all; but it was not so with me: not that I was any wiser or better than they, but be-

cause the Lord was pleased to vouchsafe me peculiar mercy, otherwise I was the most unlikely person in the ship to receive an impression, having been often before quite stupid and hardened in the very face of great dangers, and always, till this time, had hardened my neck still more and more after every reproof.—I can see no reason why the Lord singled me out for mercy but this, " that so it seemed good to him;" unless it was to shew, by one astonishing instance, that with him " nothing is im-
" possible."

There were no persons on board to whom I could open myself with freedom concerning the state of my soul, none from whom I could ask advice. As to books, I had a New Testament, Stanhope already mentioned, and a volume of Bishop Beveridge's sermons; one of which, upon our Lord's passion, affected me much.* In perusing the New Testament I was struck with several passages, particularly that of the fig-tree, *Luke* xiii. the case of St Paul, 1 *Tim*. i. but particularly the Prodigal, *Luke* xv. a case I thought that had never been so nearly exemplified as by myself—and then the goodness of the father in receiving,

nay

nay in running to meet such a son, and this intended only to illustrate the Lord's goodness to returning sinners—this gained upon me. I continued much in prayer; I saw that the Lord had interposed *so far* to save me, and I hoped he would do more. The outward circumstances helped in this place to make me still more serious and earnest in crying to him who alone could relieve me; and sometimes I thought I could be content to die even for want of food, so I might but die a believer. Thus far I was answered, that before we arrived in Ireland I had a satisfactory evidence in my own mind of the truth of the gospel, as considered in itself, and its exact suitableness to answer all my needs. I saw, that, by the way there pointed out, God might declare not his mercy only, but his justice also, in the pardon of sin, on the account of the obedience and sufferings of Jesus Christ. My judgment at that time embraced the sublime doctrine of " God " manifest in the flesh, reconciling the " world to himself." I had no idea of those systems which allow the Saviour no higher honour than that of an *upper servant*, or at the most a *demi god*. I stood in
need

need of an almighty Saviour, and such a one I found described in the New Testament. Thus far the Lord had wrought a marvellous thing; I was no longer an infidel, I heartily renounced my former profaneness; I had taken up some right notions, was seriously disposed, and sincerely touched with a sense of the undeserved mercy I had received, in being brought safe through so many dangers. I was sorry for my past misspent life, and purposed an immediate reformation: I was quite freed from the habit of swearing, which seemed to have been deeply rooted in me as a second nature. Thus, to all appearance, I was a new man.

But though I cannot doubt that this change, so far as it prevailed, was wrought by the Spirit and power of God, yet still I was greatly deficient in many respects. I was in some degree affected with a sense of my more enormous sins, but I was little aware of the innate evils of my heart. I had no apprehension of the spirituality and extent of the law of God; the hidden life of a Christian, as it consists in communion with God by Jesus Christ, and a continual dependence on him for hourly supplies of wisdom,

wisdom, strength, and comfort, was a mystery of which I had as yet no knowledge. I acknowledged the Lord's mercy in pardoning what was past, but depended chiefly upon my own resolution to do better for the time to come. I had no Christian friend or faithful minister to advise me that my strength was no more than my righteousness; and though I soon began to enquire for serious books, yet not having spiritual discernment, I frequently made a wrong choice, and I was not brought in the way of evangelical preaching or conversation (except a few times when I heard but understood not) for six years after this period. Those things the Lord was pleased to discover to me gradually. I learnt them here a little and there a little, by my own painful experience, at a distance from the common means and ordinances, and in the midst of the same course of evil company, and bad examples, as I had been conversant with for some time. From this period I could no more make a mock at sin, or jest with holy things; I no more questioned the truth of scripture, or lost a sense of the rebukes of conscience. Therefore I consider this as the beginning of my return to God, or rather of his return to me; but I cannot confider myfelf to have been a believer (in the full fenfe of the word) till a confiderable time afterwards.

I have told you, that in the time of our diftrefs we had frefh water in abundance. This was a confiderable relief to us, especially as our fpare diet was moftly falt fifh without bread; we drank plentifully, and were not afraid of wanting water; yet our ftock of this likewife was much nearer to an end than we expected: we fuppofed that we had fix large butts of water on board, and it was well that we were fafe arrived in Ireland before we difcovered that five of them were empty, having been removed out of their places, and ftove by the violent agitation when the fhip was full of water. If we had found this out while we were at fea, it would have greatly heightened our diftrefs, as we muft have drank more fparingly.

While the fhip was refitting at Lough-Swilly, I repaired to Londonderry. I lodged at an exceeding good houfe, where I was treated with much kindnefs, and foon recruited my health and ftrength. I was how-a serious professor, went twice a day to the prayers at church, and determined to receive the sacrament the next opportunity. A few days before, I signified my intention to the minister, as the rubric directs, but I found this practice was grown obsolete. At length the day came: I arose very early—was very particular and earnest in my private devotion, and with the greatest solemnity engaged myself to be the Lord's for ever, and only his. This was not a formal, but a sincere surrender, under a warm sense of mercies recently received; and yet, for want of a better knowledge of myself, and the subtilty of Satan's temptations, I was seduced to forget the vows of God that were upon me. Upon the whole, though my views of the gospel-salvation were very indistinct, I experienced a peace and satisfaction in the ordinance that day, to which I had been hitherto a perfect stranger.

The next day I was abroad with the Mayor of the city and some other gentlemen, shooting; I climbed up a steep bank, and pulling my fowling-piece after me, as I held it in a perpendicular direction, it went off so near my face as to burn away the corner of my hat.——Thus when we think ourselves in the greatest safety, we are no less exposed to danger, than when all the elements seem conspiring to destroy us. The divine Providence, which is sufficient to deliver us in our utmost extremity, is equally necessary to our preservation in the most peaceful situation.

During our stay in Ireland I wrote home. The vessel I was in had not been heard of for eighteen months, and was given up for lost long before. My father had no more expectation of hearing that I was alive, but he received my letter a few days before he left London.—He was just going Governor of York Fort in Hudson's Bay, from whence he never returned. He sailed before I landed in England, or he had purposed to take me with him; but God designing otherwise, one hindrance or other delayed us in Ireland until it was too late. I received two or three affectionate letters from him, but I never had the pleasure of seeing him more. I had hopes, that in three years more I should have had an opportunity of asking his forgiveness for the uneasiness my disobedience had given him; but the ship that was to have brought him home

came

came without him. According to the best accounts we received, he was seized with the cramp when bathing, and drowned, a little before her arrival in the bay.——— Excuse this digression.

My father, willing to contribute all in his power to my satisfaction, paid a visit before his departure to my friends in Kent, and gave his consent to the union which had been so long talked of. Thus when I returned to———, I found I had only the consent of one person to obtain; with her I as yet stood at as great an uncertainty as on the first day I saw her.

I arrived at——— the latter end of May 1748, about the same day that my father sailed from the Nore, but found the Lord had provided me another father in the gentleman whose ship had brought me home. He received me with great tenderness, and the strongest expressions of friendship and assistance; yet no more than he has since made good: for to him, as the instrument of God's goodness, I owe my all. Yet it would not have been in the power even of this friend to have served me effectually, if the Lord had not met with me on my way home, as I have related,

ted. Till then, I was like the man possessed with the *legion*.—No arguments, no per-
suasion, no views of interest, no remembrance of the past, or regard to the future,
could have constrained me within the
bounds of common prudence. But now I
was in some measure restored to my senses.
My friend immediately offered me the command of a ship; but upon mature consideration, I declined it for the present. I
had been hitherto always unsettled and
careless, and therefore thought I had better make another voyage first, and learn
to obey, and acquire a further insight and
experience in business, before I ventured
to undertake such a charge. The mate of
the vessel I came home in was preferred to
the command of a new ship, and I engaged
to go in the station of mate with him. I
made a short visit to London, &c. which
did not fully answer my views. I had but
one opportunity of seeing Mrs N******,
of which I availed myself very little, for I
was always exceeding aukward in pleading
my own cause *viva voce*.—— But after my
return to L———, I put the question in
such a manner, by letter, that she could
not avoid (unless I had greatly mistaken
her)

her) coming to some sort of an explanation. Her answer (though penned with abundance of caution), satisfied me, as I collected from it, that she was free from any other engagement, and not unwilling to wait the event of the voyage I had undertaken. I should be ashamed to trouble you with these little details, if you had not yourself desired me.

I am,

Yours, &c.

January 20, 1763.

LETTER

LETTER X.

Dear Sir,

MY connections with sea-affairs have often led me to think, that the varieties observable in Christian experience may be properly illustrated from the circumstances of a voyage. Imagine to yourself a number of vessels, at different times, and from different places, bound to the same port; there are some things in which all these would agree—the compass steered by the port in view, the general rules of navigation, both as to the management of the vessel, and determining their astronomical observation, would be the same in all. In other respects they would differ: perhaps no two of them would meet with the same distribution of winds and weather. Some we see set out with a prosperous gale, and when they almost think their passage secured, they are checked by adverse blasts; and after enduring much hardship and danger, and frequent expectations of shipwreck, they just escape, and
reach

reach the desired haven. Others meet the greatest difficulties at first; they put forth in a storm, and are often beaten back; at length their voyage proves favourable, and they enter the port with a πληροφορια, a rich and abundant entrance. Some are hard beset with cruisers and enemies, and obliged to fight their way through; others meet with little remarkable in their passage. Is it not thus in the spiritual life? All true believers walk by the same rule, and mind the same things: The word of God is their compass, JESUS is both their polar star and their sun of righteousness; their hearts and faces are all set Sion-ward. Thus far they are as one body, animated by one Spirit; yet their experience, formed upon these common principles, is far from uniform. The Lord, in his first call, and his following dispensations, has a regard to the situation, temper, talents of each, and to the particular services or trials he has appointed them for. Though all are exercised at times, yet some pass through the voyage of life much more smoothly than others. But he, "who walks upon the wings of "the wind, and measures the waters in "the hollow of his hand," will not suffer

any

any of whom he has once taken charge, to perish in the storms, though for a season, perhaps, many of them are ready to give up all hopes.

We must not therefore make the experience of others, in all respects, a rule to ourselves, nor our own a rule to others; yet these are common mistakes, and productive of many more. As to myself, every part of my case has been extraordinary. —I have hardly met a single instance resembling it. Few, very few, have been recovered from such a dreadful state; and the few that have been thus favoured, have generally passed through the most severe convictions; and after the Lord has given them peace, their future lives have been usually more zealous, bright, and exemplary than common. Now, as on the one hand my convictions were very moderate, and far below what might have been expected from the dreadful review I had to make, so, on the other, my first beginnings in a religious course were as faint as can be well imagined. I never knew that season alluded to, *Jer.* ii. 2. *Rev.* ii. 4. usually called *the time of the first love.* Who would not expect to hear, that after such a wonderful

derful unhoped-for deliverance as I had received, and after my eyes were in some measure enlightened to see things aright, I should immediately cleave to the Lord and his ways, with full purpose of heart, and consult no more with flesh and blood? But, alas! it was far otherwise with me. I had learned to pray; I set some value upon the word of God, and was no longer a libertine; but my soul still cleaved to the dust. Soon after my departure from L——, I began to intermit, and grow slack in waiting upon the Lord; I grew vain and trifling in my conversation; and though my heart smote me often, yet my armour was gone, and I declined fast; and by the time I arrived at Guinea, I seemed to have forgot all the Lord's mercies, and my own engagements, and was (profaneness excepted) almost as bad as before. The enemy prepared a train of temptations, and I became his easy prey; and, for about a month, he lulled me asleep in a course of evil, of which, a few months before, I could not have supposed myself any longer capable. How much propriety is there in the apostle's advice, " Take heed, lest any of " you be hardened through the deceitful-
" ness

"ness of sin." O who can be sufficiently upon their guard! Sin first deceives, and then it hardens: I was now fast bound in chains; I had little desire, and no power at all to recover myself. I could not but at times reflect how it was with me; but if I attempted to struggle with it, it was in vain. I was just like Samson, when he said, "I will go forth, and shake myself as "at other times;" but the Lord was departed, and he found himself helpless, in the hands of his enemies. By the remembrance of this interval, the Lord has often instructed me since, what a poor creature I am in myself, incapable of standing a single hour, without continual fresh supplies of strength and grace from the fountain-head.

At length the Lord, whose mercies are infinite, interposed in my behalf. My business in this voyage, while upon the coast, was to sail from place to place in the long-boat to purchase slaves. The ship was at Sierra Leon, and I then at the Plantanes, the scene of my former captivity, where every thing I saw might seem to remind me of my ingratitude. I was in easy circumstances, courted by those who formerly despised

spised me: the *lime-trees* I had planted were growing tall, and promised fruit the following year, against which time I had expectations of returning with a ship of my own. But none of these things affected me, till, as I have said, the Lord again interposed to save me. He visited me with a violent fever, which broke the fatal chain, and once more brought me to myself. But O what a prospect! I thought myself now summoned away——My past dangers and deliverances, my earnest prayers in the time of trouble, my solemn vows before the Lord at his table, and my ungrateful returns for all his goodness, were all present to my mind at once. Then I began to wish that the Lord had suffered me to sink into the ocean, when I first besought his mercy. For a little while I concluded the door of hope to be quite shut; but this continued not long. Weak, and almost delirious, I arose from my bed, and crept to a retired part of the island, and here I found a renewed liberty to pray. I durst make no more resolves, but cast myself before the Lord, to do with me as he should please. I do not remember that any particular text, or remarkable discovery, was presented to

L my

my mind, but in general I was enabled to hope and believe in a crucified Saviour. The burden was removed from my confcience, and not only my peace, but my health was reftored; I cannot fay inftantaneoufly, but I recovered from that hour, and fo faft, that when I returned to the fhip two days afterwards, I was perfectly well before I got on board. And from that time, I truft, I have been delivered from the power and dominion of fin, though as to the effects and conflicts of fin dwelling in me, I ftill " groan, being burden-" ed." I now began again to wait upon the Lord; and though I have often grieved his Spirit, and foolifhly wandered from him fince, (when, alas, fhall I be more wife!), yet his powerful grace has hitherto preferved me from fuch black declenfions as this I have laft recorded; and I humbly truft in his mercy and promifes, that he will be my guide and guard to the end.

My leifure hours in this voyage were chiefly employed in learning the Latin language, which I had now entirely forgot. This defire took place from an imitation I had feen of one of Horace's odes in a magazine. I began the attempt under the

greateft

greatest disadvantages possible; for I pitched upon a poet, perhaps the most difficult of the poets, even Horace himself, for my first book. I had picked up an old English translation of him, which, with Castalio's Latin Bible, were all my helps. I forgot a Dictionary, but I would not therefore give up my purpose. I had the edition *in usum Delphini*; and by comparing the Odes with the interpretation, and tracing the words, I could understand from one place to another by the index, with the assistance I could get from the Latin Bible: in this way, by dint of hard industry, often waking when I might have slept, I made some progress before I returned, and not only understood the sense and meaning of many Odes, and some of the Epistles, but began to relish the beauties of the composition, and acquired a spice of what Mr Law calls *classical enthusiasm*. And indeed, by this means, I had Horace more *ad unguem* than some who are masters of the Latin tongue; for my helps were so few, that I generally had the passage fixed in my memory, before I could fully understand its meaning.

My business in the long-boat, during eight

eight months we were upon the coast, exposed me to innumerable dangers and perils, from burning suns and chilling dews, winds, rains, and thunder-storms, in the open boat; and on shore, from long journies through the woods, and the temper of the natives, who are in many places cruel, treacherous, and watching opportunities for mischief. Several boats in the same time were cut off, several white men poisoned, and in my own boat I buried six or seven people with fevers. When going on shore, or returning from it, in their little canoes, I have been more than once or twice overset by the violence of the surf, or beach of the sea, and brought to land half dead, (for I could not swim). An account of such escapes as I still remember, would swell to several sheets, and many more I have perhaps forgot; I shall only select one instance, as a specimen of that wonderful providence which watched over me for good, and which, I doubt not, you will think worthy of notice.

When our trade was finished, and we were near sailing to the West Indies, the only remaining service I had to perform in the boat, was to assist in bringing the
wood

wood and water from the shore. We were then at Rio Sestors. I used to go into the river in the afternoon with the sea-breeze, procure my loading in the evening, and return on board in the morning with the land wind. Several of these little voyages I had made, but the boat was grown old, and almost unfit for use. This service likewise was almost completed. One day having dined on board, I was preparing to return to the river as formerly: I had taken leave of the Captain, received his orders, was ready in the boat, and just going to put off, as we term it, that is, to let go our ropes, and sail from the ship. In that instant the Captain came up from the cabin, and called me on board again.——I went, expecting further orders; but he said, he had *took it in his head,* (as he phrased it), that I should remain that day in the ship, and accordingly ordered another man to go in my room. I was surprised at this, as the boat had never been sent away without me before, and asked him the reason; he could give me no reason but as above, that so he would have it. Accordingly the boat went without me, but returned no more. She sunk that night in the river, and the perfon who had fupplied my place was drowned. I was much ftruck when we received news of the event the next morning.—The Captain himfelf, though quite a ftranger to religion, fo far as to deny a particular Providence, could not help being affected; but he declared, that he had no other reafon for countermanding me at that time, but that it came fuddenly into his mind to detain me.—— I wonder I omitted this in my eight letters, as I have always thought it one of the moft extraordinary circumftances of my life.

  I am,

   Dear Sir,

     Your obliged fervant.

January 21. 1763.

LETTER

LETTER XI.

Dear Sir,

A Few days after I was thus wonderfully saved from an unforeseen danger, we sailed for Antigua, and from thence proceeded to Charlestown in South Carolina. In this place there are many serious people, but I knew not where to find them out; indeed I was not aware of a difference, but supposed that all who attended public worship were good Christians. I was as much in the dark about preaching, not doubting but whatever came from the pulpit must be very good. I had two or three opportunities of hearing a dissenting minister named Smith, who, by what I have known since, I believe to have been an excellent and powerful preacher of the gospel; and there was something in his manner that struck me, but I did not rightly understand him. The best words that men can speak are ineffectual till explained and applied by the Spirit of God, who alone can open the heart. It pleased the

Lord

Lord for some time that I should learn no more than what he enabled me to collect from my own experience and reflection. my conduct was now very inconsistent— Almost every day, when business would permit, I used to retire into the woods and fields, (for these, when at hand, have always been my favourite oratories), and I trust I began to taste the sweets of communion with God in the exercises of prayer and praise, and yet I frequently spent the evenings in vain and worthless company; indeed my relish for worldly diversions was much weakened, and I was rather a spectator than a sharer in their pleasures, but I did not as yet see the necessity of an absolute forbearance. Yet as my compliance with custom and company was chiefly owing to want of light, rather than to an obstinate attachment, and the Lord was pleased to preserve me from what I *knew* was sinful, I had for the most part peace of conscience, and my strongest desires were towards the things of God. As yet I knew not the force of that precept, " Abstain " from all appearance of evil;"—but very often ventured upon the brink of temptation; but the Lord was gracious to my weakness

weakness, and would not suffer the enemy to prevail against me. I did not break with the world at once, (as might in my case have been expected), but I was gradually led to see the inconvenience and folly of one thing after another, and when I saw it, the Lord strengthened me to give it up. But it was some years before I was set quite at liberty from occasional compliances in many things in which at this time I durst by no means allow myself.

We finished our voyage, and arrived in L⸺. When the ship's affairs were settled I went to London, and from thence (as you may suppose) I soon repaired to Kent. More than seven years were now elapsed since my first visit—No views of the kind could seem more chimerical, or could subsist under greater discouragements than mine had done; yet, through the over-ruling goodness of God, while I seemed abandoned to myself, and blindly following my own head-strong passions, I was guided by a hand that I knew not, to the accomplishment of my wishes. Every obstacle was now removed. I had renounced my former follies, my interest was established, and friends on all sides consenting;

senting; the point was now entirely between ourselves, and, after what had past, was easily concluded.——Accordingly our hands were joined on the 1st of February 1750.

The satisfaction I have found in this union, you will suppose has been greatly heightened by reflection on the former disagreeable contrasts I had passed through, and the views I have had of the singular mercy and providence of the Lord in bringing it to pass. If you please to look back to the beginning of my sixth letter, (page 71), I doubt not but you will allow that few persons have known more, either of the misery or happiness of which human life (as considered in itself) is capable. How easily, at a time of life when I was so little capable of judging, (but a few months more than seventeen), might my affections have been fixed where they could have met with no return, or where success would have been the heaviest disappointment. The long delay I met with was likewise a mercy; for had I succeeded a year or two sooner, before the Lord was pleased to change my heart, we must have been mutually unhappy, even as to the present

present life. "Surely mercy and goodness "have followed me all my days."

But, alas, I soon began to feel that my heart was still hard and ungrateful to the God of my life. This crowning mercy, which raised me to all I could ask or wish in a temporal view, and which ought to have been an animating motive to obedience and praise, had a contrary effect.—I rested in the gift, and forgot the Giver. My poor narrow heart was *satisfied*—A cold and careless frame, as to spiritual things, took place, and gained ground daily. Happy for me, the season was advancing, and in June I received orders to repair to L——. This roused me from my dream; I need not tell you that I found the pains of absence and separation fully proportioned to my preceding pleasure. It was hard, very hard, to part, especially as conscience interfered, and suggested to me how little I deserved that we should be spared to meet again—But the Lord supported me. —I was a poor faint idolatrous creature; but I had now some acquaintance with the way of access to a throne of grace by the blood of Jesus, and peace was soon restored to my conscience. Yet through all the following

following voyage my irregular and excessive affections were as thorns in my eyes, and often made my other blessings tasteless and insipid. But he who doth all things well, over-ruled this likewise for good. It became an occasion of quickening me in prayer both for her and myself; it increased my indifference for company and amusement; it habituated me to a kind of voluntary self-denial, which I was afterwards taught to improve to a better purpose.

While I remained in England, we corresponded every post; and all the while I used the sea afterwards, I constantly kept up the practice of writing two or three times a week (if weather and business permitted), though no conveyance homeward offered for six or eight months together. My packets were usually heavy, and as not one of them at any time miscarried, I have to the amount of near 200 sheets of paper now lying in my bureau of that correspondence. I mention this little relief I contrived to soften the intervals of absence, because it had a good effect beyond my first intention. It habituated me to think and write upon a great variety of subjects,

subjects, and I acquired, insensibly, a greater readiness of expressing myself than I should have otherwise attained. As I gained more ground in religious knowledge, my letters became more serious, and at times I still find an advantage in looking them over, especially as they remind me of many providential incidents, and the state of my mind at different periods in these voyages, which would otherwise have escaped my memory.

I sailed from L—— in August 1750, commander of a good ship. I have no very extraordinary events to recount from this period, and shall therefore contract my memoirs, lest I become tedious; yet I am willing to give you a brief sketch of my history down to 1755, the year of my settlement in my present situation. I had now the command and care of thirty persons; I endeavoured to treat them with humanity, and to set them a good example; I likewise established public worship, according to the liturgy, twice every Lord's day, officiating myself. Farther than this I did not proceed while I continued in that employment.

Having now much leisure, I prosecuted the

the study of the Latin with good success. I remembered a dictionary this voyage, and procured two or three other books; but still it was my hap to chuse the hardest. —I added *Juvenal* to *Horace*, and for prose authors, I pitched upon *Livy*, *Cæsar*, and *Sallust*. You will easily conceive, Sir, that I had hard work to begin (where I should have left off) with *Horace* and *Livy*. I was not aware of the difference of style; I had heard *Livy* highly commended, and was resolved to understand him. I began with the first page, and laid down a rule, which I seldom departed from, not to proceed to a second period till I understood the first, and so on. I was often at a stand, but seldom discouraged: here and there I found a few lines quite obstinate, and was forced to break in upon my rule, and give them up, especially as my edition had only the text, without any notes to assist me. But there were not many such; for before the close of that voyage, I could (with a few exceptions) read *Livy* from end to end, almost as readily as an English author. And I found, in surmounting this difficulty, I had surmounted all in one. Other prose authors, when they came in my way, cost me me little trouble. In short, in the space of two or three voyages, I became tolerably acquainted with the best classics (I put all I have to say upon this subject together). I read *Terence*, *Virgil*, and several pieces of *Cicero*, and the modern classics, *Buchanan*, *Erasmus*, and *Cassimir*; at length I conceived a design of becoming *Ciceronian* myself, and thought it would be a fine thing indeed to write pure and elegant Latin.—I made some essays towards it, but by this time the Lord was pleased to draw me nearer to himself, and to give me a fuller view of the "pearl of great price," the inestimable treasure hid in the field of the holy scripture; and for the sake of this, I was made willing to part with all my new acquired riches. I began to think that life was too short (especially my life) to admit of leisure for such elaborate trifling. Neither poet or historian could tell me a word of Jesus, and I therefore applied myself to those who could. The classics were at first restrained to one morning in the week, and at length quite laid aside. I have not looked in *Livy* these five years, and I suppose I could not now well understand him. Some passages in *Horace* and

Virgil I still admire, but they seldom come in my way. I prefer *Buchanan's* psalms to a whole shelf of *Elzevirs*—But thus much I have gained, and more than this I am not solicitous about, so much of the Latin as enables me to read any useful or curious book that is published in that language. About the same time, and for the same reason that I quarrelled with *Livy*, I laid aside the mathematics.—I found they not only cost me much time, but engrossed my thoughts too far; my head was literally full of *schemes*. I was weary of cold contemplative truths, which can neither warm nor amend the heart, but rather tend to aggrandize *self*. I found no traces of this wisdom in the life of Jesus, or the writings of Paul. I do not regret that I have had some opportunities of knowing the first principles of these things, but I see much cause to praise the Lord that he inclined me to stop in time, and, whilst I was " spending my labours for that " which is not bread," was pleased to set before me " wine and milk without money " and without price."

My first voyage was fourteen months, through various scenes of danger and difficulty,

culty, but nothing very remarkable; and, as I intend to be more particular with regard to the second, I shall only say that I was preserved from every harm, and having seen many fall on my right hand and on my left, I was brought home in peace, and restored to where my thoughts had been often directed, November 2. 1751.

I am,

Sir,

Yours.

January 22. 1763.

LETTER XII.

Dear Sir,

I Almost wish I could recal my last sheet, and retract my promise. I fear I have engaged too far, and shall prove a mere *Egotist*. What have I more that can deserve your notice? However, it is some satisfaction that I am now writing to yourself only; and I believe you will have candour to excuse what nothing but a sense of your kindness could extort from me.

Soon after the period where my last closes, that is, in the interval between my first and second voyage after my marriage, I began to keep a sort of diary, a practice which I have since found of great use. I had in this interval repeated proofs of the ingratitude and evil of my heart. A life of ease, in the midst of my friends, and the full satisfaction of my wishes, was not favourable to the progress of grace, and afforded cause of daily humiliation. Yet, upon the whole, I gained ground. I became acquainted with books, which gave me a farther view of Christian doctrine and experience, particularly, *Scougal's Life of God in the Soul of Man*, *Hervey's Meditations*, and *The Life of Colonel Gairdner*. As to preaching, I heard none but the common sort, and had hardly an idea of any better; neither had I the advantage of Christian acquaintance. I was likewise greatly hindered by a cowardly reserved spirit; I was afraid of being thought precise, and though I could not live without prayer, I durst not propose it even to my wife, till she herself first put me upon it; so far was I from those expressions of zeal and love, which seem so suitable to the case of one who has had much forgiven. In a few months the returning season called me abroad again, and I sailed from L—— in a new ship, July 1752.

A seafaring life is necessarily excluded from the benefit of public ordinances and Christian communion; but, as I have observed, my loss upon these heads was at this time but small. In other respects, I know not any calling that seems more favourable, or affords greater advantages to an awakened mind, for promoting the life of God in the soul, especially to a person who

who has the command of a ship, and thereby has it in his power to restrain gross irregularities in others, and to dispose of his own time; and still more so in African voyages, as these ships carry a double proportion of men and officers to most others, which made my department very easy; and, excepting the hurry of trade, &c. upon the coast, which is rather occasional than constant, afforded me abundance of leisure. To be at sea in these circumstances, withdrawn out of the reach of innumerable temptations, with opportunity and a turn of mind disposed to observe the wonders of God in the great deep, with the two noblest objects of sight, the expanded *heavens*, and the expanded *ocean* continually in view, and where evident interpositions of divine providence, in answer to prayer, occur almost every day; these are helps to quicken and confirm the life of faith, which, in a good measure, supply to a religious sailor the want of those advantages which can be only enjoyed upon the shore. And indeed, though my knowledge of spiritual things (as knowledge is usually estimated) was at this time very small, yet I sometimes look back with regret

regret upon those scenes. I never knew sweeter or more frequent hours of divine communion, than in my two last voyages to Guinea, when I was either almost secluded from society on ship-board, or when on shore amongst the natives. I have wandered through the woods, reflecting on the singular goodness of the Lord to me, in a place where, perhaps, there was not a person that knew him for some thousand miles round me. Many a time, upon these occasions, I have restored the beautiful lines of Propertius to their right owner; lines full of blasphemy and madness, when addressed to a creature, but full of comfort and propriety in the mouth of a believer.

Sic ego desertis possim bene vivere sylvis
Quo nulla humano sit via trita pede:
Tu mihi curarum requies, in nocte velatra
Lumen, et in solis tu mihi turba locis.

PARAPHRASED.

In desert woods with thee, my God,
Where human footsteps never trod,
    How happy could I be!
Thou my repose from care, my light
Amidst the darkness of the night,
    In solitude my company.

In the course of this voyage I was wonderfully preserved in the midst of many obvious and many unforeseen dangers. At one time there was a conspiracy amongst my own people to turn pirates, and take the ship from me. When the plot was nearly ripe, and they only waited a convenient opportunity, two of those concerned in it were taken ill one day; one of them died, and he was the only person I buried while on board. This suspended the affair, and opened a way to its discovery, or the consequence might have been fatal. The slaves on board were likewise frequently plotting insurrections, and were sometimes upon the very brink of mischief; but it was always disclosed in due time. When I have thought myself most secure, I have been suddenly alarmed with danger; and when I have almost despaired of life, as sudden a deliverance has been vouchsafed me. My stay upon the coast was long, the trade very precarious, and in the pursuit of my business, both on board and on shore, I was *in deaths often.* Let the following instance serve as a specimen.

I was at a place called *Mana*, near Cape Mount, where I had transacted very large concerns,

concerns, and had, at the time I am speaking of, some debts and accounts to settle, which required my attendance on shore, and I intended to go as the next morning. When I arose, I left the ship, according to my purpose; but when I came near the shore, the surf, or breach of the sea, ran so high, that I was almost afraid to attempt landing. Indeed I had often ventured at a worse time, but I felt an inward hindrance and backwardness, which I could not account for: the surf furnished a pretext for indulging it, and after waiting and hesitating for about half an hour, I returned to the ship, without doing my business, which I think I never did, but that morning, in all the time I used that trade. —But I soon perceived the reason of all this.—It seems, the day before I intended to land, a scandalous and groundless charge had been laid against me, (by whose instigation I could never learn), which greatly threatened my honour and interest both in Africa and England, and would perhaps, humanly speaking, have affected my life, if I had landed according to my intention. I shall perhaps inclose a letter, which will give a full account of this strange adventure,

ture, and therefore shall say no more of it here, any further than to tell you, that an attempt, aimed to destroy either my life or character, and which might very probably, in it consequences, have ruined my voyage, passed off without the least inconvenience. The person most concerned, owed me about a hundred pounds, which he sent me in a huff, and otherwise, perhaps, would not have paid me at all. I was very uneasy for a few hours, but was soon afterwards comforted. I heard no more of my accusation till the next voyage, and then it was publicly acknowledged to be a malicious calumny, without the least shadow of a ground.

Such was the vicissitudes and difficulties through which the Lord preserved me. Now and then both faith and patience were sharply exercised, but suitable strength was given; and as those things did not occur every day, the study of the Latin, of which I gave a general account in my last, was renewed, and carried on from time to time, when business would permit. I was mostly very regular in the management of my time; I allotted eight hours for sleep and meals, eight hours for exercise and devotion,

votion, and eight hours to my books: and thus, by diversifying my engagements, the whole day was agreeably filled up, and I seldom found a day too long, or an hour to spare. My studies kept me employed, and so far it was well; otherwise they were hardly worth the time they cost, as they led me to an admiration of false models and false maxims; an almost unavoidable consequence (I suppose) of an admiration of classic authors. Abating what I have attained of the language, I think I might have read *Cassandra* or *Cleopatra* to as good purpose as I read *Livy*, whom I now account an equal *romancer*, though in a different way.

From the coast I went to St Christophers; and here my idolatrous heart was its own punishment. The letters I expected from Mrs N****** were by mistake forwarded to Antigua, which had been at first proposed as our port. As I was certain of her punctuality in writing, if alive, I concluded, by not hearing from her, that she was surely dead. This fear affected me more and more; I lost my appetite and rest; I felt an incessant pain in my stomach, and in about three weeks time I was

neat sinking under the weight of an imaginary stroke. I felt some severe symptoms of that mixture of pride and madness which is commonly called *a broken heart*; and indeed I wonder that this case is not more common than it appears to be. How often do the potsherds of the earth presume to contend with their Maker! and what a wonder of mercy is it that they are not all broken! However, my complaint was not all grief; conscience had a share. I thought my unfaithfulness to God had deprived me of her, especially my backwardness in speaking of spiritual things, which I could hardly attempt, even to her. It was this thought, that I had lost invaluable, irrecoverable opportunities, which both duty and affection should have engaged me to improve, that chiefly stung me; and I thought I would have given the world to know she was living, (that I might at least discharge my engagements by writing), though I was never to see her again. This was a sharp lesson, but I hope it did me good; and when I had thus suffered some weeks, I thought of sending a small vessel to Antigua. I did so, and she brought me several packets, which restored my
health

health and peace, and gave me a strong contrast of the Lord's goodness to me, and my unbelief and ingratitude towards him.

In August 1753 I returned to L———. My stay was very short at home that voyage, only six weeks; in that space nothing very memorable occurred; I shall therefore begin my next with an account of my third and last voyage. And thus I give both you and myself hopes of a speedy period to these Memoirs, which begin to be tedious and minute even to myself; only I am animated by the thought that I write at your request, and have therefore an opportunity of shewing myself

Your obliged servant,

January 31. 1763.

LETTER XIII.

Dear Sir,

MY third voyage was shorter and less perplexed than either of the former. Before I sailed, I met with a young man who had formerly been a midshipman, and my intimate companion on board the Harwich. He was, at the time I first knew him, a sober youth, but I found too much success in my unhappy attempts to infect him with libertine principles. When we met at L——, our acquaintance renewed upon the ground of our former intimacy. He had good sense, and had read many books.—Our conversation frequently turned upon religion, and I was very desirous to repair the mischief I had done him. I gave him a plain account of the manner and reason of my change, and used every argument to persuade him to relinquish his infidel schemes; and when I sometimes pressed him so close that he had no other reply to make, he would remind me that I was the very first person who had given

him

him an idea of his liberty. This occasioned me many mournful reflections. He was then going master to Guinea himself; but before his ship was ready, his merchant became a bankrupt, which disconcerted his voyage. As he had no farther expectations for that year, I offered to take him with me as a companion, that he might gain a knowledge of the coast, and the gentlemen who employed me promised to provide for him upon his return. My view in this was not so much to serve him in his business, as to have an opportunity of debating the point with him at leisure; and I hoped, in the course of my voyage, my arguments, example, and prayers, might have some good effect on him. My intention in this step was better than my judgment, and I had frequent reason to repent it. He was exceedingly profane, and grew worse and worse. I saw in him a most lively picture of what I had once been, but it was very inconvenient to have it always before my eyes. Besides, he was not only deaf to my remonstrances himself, but laboured all he could to counteract my influence upon others. His spirit and passions were likewise exceeding high, so that it required all my prudence and authority to hold him in any degree of restraint. He was as a sharp thorn in my side for some time; but at length I had an opportunity upon the coast of buying a small vessel, which I supplied with a cargo from my own, and gave him the command, and sent him away to trade on the ship's account. When we parted, I repeated and enforced my best advice. I believe his friendship and regard was as great as could be expected, where principles were so diametrically opposite; he seemed greatly affected when I left him, but my words had no weight with him; when he found himself at liberty from under my eye, he gave a hasty loose to every appetite; and his violent irregularities, joined to the heat of the climate, soon threw him into a malignant fever, which carried him off in a few days. He died convinced, but not changed. The account I had from those who were with him was dreadful; his rage and despair struck them all with horror, and he pronounced his own fatal doom before he expired, without any appearance that he either *hoped* or *asked* for mercy. I thought this awful contrast might not be improper to give you, as a

stronger

stronger view of the distinguishing goodness of God to me, the chief of sinners.

I left the coast in about four months, and sailed for St Christophers. Hitherto I had enjoyed a perfect state of health, equally in every climate, for several years; but upon this passage I was visited with a fever, which gave me a very near prospect of eternity. I have obtained liberty to inclose you three or four letters, which will more clearly illustrate the state and measure of my experience at different times, than any thing I can say at present. One of them, you will find, was wrote at this period, when I could hardly hold a pen, and had some reason to believe I should write no more. I had not that πληροφορια * which is so desirable at a time when flesh and heart fails; but my hopes were greater than my fears, and I felt a silent composure of spirit, which enabled me to wait the event without much anxiety. My trust, though weak in degree, was alone fixed upon the blood and righteousness of Jesus, and those words, "he is able to save to the "uttermost," gave me great relief.——I was for a while troubled with a very sin-

* Full assurance.

gular thought; whether it was a temptation, or that the fever diforderd my faculties, I cannot fay; but I feemed not fo much afraid of wrath and punifhment, as of being loft and overlooked amidft the myriads that are continually entering the unfeen world. What is my foul (thought I), amongft fuch an innumerable multitude of beings.———And this troubled me greatly. Perhaps the Lord will take no notice of me. I was perplexed thus for fome time, but at laft a text of fcripture, very appofite to the cafe, occurred to my mind, and put an end to the doubt, " The " Lord knoweth them that are his." In about ten days, beyond the hopes of thofe about me, I began to amend, and by the time of our arrival in the Weft Indies, I was perfectly recovered.———I hope this vifitation was made ufeful to me.

Thus far, that is, for about the fpace of fix years, the Lord was pleafed to lead me in a fecret way.———I had learned fomething of the evil of my heart; I had read the Bible over and over, with feveral good books, and had a general view of the *gofpel-truth*; but my conceptions were, in many refpects, confufed, not having in all this

this time met with one acquaintance who could affist my inquiries. But upon my arrival at St Chriftophers this voyage, I found a Captain of a fhip from London, whofe converfation was greatly helpful to me. He was and is a member of Mr B———r's church, a man of experience in the things of God, and of a lively communicative turn. We difcovered each other by fome cafual expreffions in mixed company, and foon became (fo far as bufinefs would permit) infeparable. For near a month we fpent every evening together on board each other's fhip alternately, and often prolonged our vifits till towards day-break. I was all ears; and what was better, he not only informed my underftanding, but his difcourfe inflamed my heart.——He encouraged me to open my mouth in focial prayer; he taught me the advantage of Chriftian converfe; he put me upon an attempt to make my profeffion more public, and to venture to fpeak for God. From him, or rather from the Lord by his means, I received an increafe of knowledge: my conceptions became clearer and more evangelical, and I was delivered from a fear which had long troubled me, the

fear

fear of relapsing into my former apostasy. But now I began to understand the security of the covenant of grace, and to expect to be preserved, not by my own power and holiness, but by the mighty power and promise of God, through faith in an unchangeable Saviour. He likewise gave me a general view of the state of religion, with the errors and controversies of the times, (things to which I had been entirely a stranger), and finally directed me where to apply in London for further instruction. With these new-acquired advantages I left him, and my passage homewards gave me leisure to digest what I had received: I had much comfort and freedom during those seven weeks, and my sun was seldom clouded. I arrived safe in L———, August 1754.

My stay at home was intended to be but short, and by the beginning of November I was again ready for the sea; but the Lord saw fit to over-rule my design. During the time I was engaged in the slave-trade, I never had the least scruple as to its lawfulness; I was upon the whole satisfied with it, as the appointment Providence had marked out for me; yet it was, in many respects, far from eligible. It is indeed

accounted

accounted a genteel employment, and is usually very profitable, though to me it did not prove so, the Lord seeing that a large increase of wealth would not be good for me. However, I considered myself as a sort of *goaler* or *turnkey*; and I was sometimes shocked with an employment that was perpetually conversant with chains, bolts, and shackles. In this view I had often petitioned in my prayers, that the Lord (in his own time) would be pleased to fix me in a more humane calling, and (if it might be) place me where I might have more frequent converse with his people and ordinances, and be freed from those long separations from home, which very often were hard to bear. My prayers were now answered, though in a way I little expected. I now experienced another sudden unforeseen change of life. I was within two days of sailing, and to all appearance in good health as usual; but in the afternoon, as I was sitting with Mrs N*****, by ourselves, drinking tea, and talking over past events, I was in a moment seized with a fit, which deprived me of sense and motion, and left me no other sign of life, than that of breathing.——I suppose it
was

was of the apoplectic kind—It lasted about an hour, and when I recovered, it left a pain and dizziness in my head, which continued with such symptoms as induced the physicians to judge it would not be safe or prudent for me to proceed on the voyage. Accordingly, by the advice of my friend to whom the ship belonged, I resigned the command the day before she sailed; and thus I was unexpectedly called from that service, and freed from a share of the future consequences of that voyage, which proved extremely calamitous. The person who went in my room, most of the officers, and many of the crew, died, and the vessel was brought home with great difficulty.

As I was now disengaged from business, I left L——, and spent most of the following year at London and in Kent. But I entered upon a new trial.——You will easily conceive that Mrs N***** was not an unconcerned spectator when I lay extended, and, as she thought, expiring upon the ground. In effect, the blow that struck me reached her in the same instant: she did not indeed immediately feel it, till her apprehensions on my account began to subside;

but

but as I grew better, she became worse: her surprize threw her into a disorder which no physicians could define, or medicines remove. Without any of the ordinary symptoms of a consumption, she decayed almost visibly, till she became so weak, that she could hardly bear any one to walk across the room she was in. I was placed for about eleven months in what Dr Young calls the

———dreadful post of observation,
Darker every hour.

It was not till after my settlement in my present station that the Lord was pleased to restore her by his own hand, when all hopes from ordinary means were at an end. But before this took place, I have some other particulars to mention, which must be the subject of the following sheet, which I hope will be the last on this subject, from

Your affectionate servant.

February 1. 1763.

LETTER

LETTER XIV.

Dear Sir,

BY the directions I had received from my friend at St Kitts, I soon found out a religious acquaintance in London. I first applied to Mr B――, and chiefly attended upon his ministry, when in town. From him I received many helps, both in public and private; for he was pleased to favour me with his friendship from the first. His kindness, and the intimacy between us, has continued and increased to this day; and of all my many friends, I am most deeply indebted to him. The late Mr H――d was my second acquaintance, a man of a choice spirit, and an abundant zeal for the Lord's service. I enjoyed his correspondence till near the time of his death. Soon after, upon Mr W――d's return from America, my two good friends introduced me to him; and though I had little personal acquaintance with him till afterwards, his ministry was exceeding useful to me. I had likewise access to some

religious

religious societies, and became known to many excellent Christians in private life. Thus, when at London, I lived at the fountain-head, as it were, for spiritual advantages. When I was in Kent it was very different, yet I found some serious persons there; but the fine variegated woodland country afforded me advantages of another kind. Most of my time, at least some hours every day, I passed in retirement, when the weather was fair; sometimes in the thickest woods, sometimes on the highest hills, where almost every step varied the prospect. It has been my custom, for many years, to perform my devotional exercises *sub dio*, when I have opportunity, and I always find these rural scenes have some tendency both to refresh and to compose my spirits. A beautiful diversified prospect gladdens my heart. When I am withdrawn from the noise and petty works of men, I consider myself as in the great temple which the Lord has built for his own honour.

The country between Rochester and Maidstone, bordering upon the Medway, was well suited to the turn of my mind; and was I to go over it now, I could point to many a place where I remember to have either earnestly sought, or happily found the Lord's comfortable presence with my soul. And thus I lived sometimes at London, and sometimes in the country, till the autumn of the following year. All this while I had two trials more or less upon my mind: the first and principal was Mrs N****'s illness; she still grew worse, and I had daily more reason to fear that the hour of separation was at hand. When faith was in exercise, I was in some measure resigned to the Lord's will; but too often my heart rebelled, and I found it hard either to trust or to submit. I had likewise some care about my future settlement; the African trade was overdone that year, and my friends did not care to fit out another ship till mine returned. I was some time in suspense, but indeed a provision of food and raiment has seldom been a cause of great sollicitude to me. I found it easier to trust the Lord in this point than in the former, and accordingly this was first answered. In August I received an account, that I was nominated to the office of ———. These places are usually obtained, or at least sought,

by

by dint of much interest and application; but this came to me unsought and unexpected. I knew, indeed, my good friend in L—— had endeavoured to procure another post for me, but found it pre-engaged. I found afterwards, that the place I had missed would have been very unsuitable for me, and that this, which I had no thought of, was the very thing I could have wished for, afforded me much leisure, and the liberty of living in my own way. Several circumstances, unnoticed by others, concurred to shew me, that the good hand of the Lord was as remarkably concerned in this event, as in any other leading turn of my life.

But when I gained this point, my distress in the other was doubled: I was obliged to leave Mrs N***** in the greatest extremity of pain and illness, when the physicians could do no more, and I had no ground of hope that I should see her again alive, but this—that nothing is impossible with the Lord. I had a severe conflict, but faith prevailed: I found the promise remarkably fulfilled, of strength proportioned to my need. The day before I set out, and not till then, the burden was entirely

tirely taken from my mind; I was strengthened to resign both her and myself to the Lord's disposal, and departed from her in a chearful frame. Soon after I was gone she began to amend, and recovered so fast, that in about two months I had the pleasure to meet her at Stone, on her journey to L——.

And now I think I have answered, if not exceeded, your desire. Since October 1755, we have been comfortably settled here, and all my circumstances have been as remarkably smooth and uniform, as they were various in former years. My trials have been light and few—not but that I still find, in the experience of every day, the necessity of a life of faith. My principal trial is— the body of sin and death, which makes me often to sigh out the apostle's complaint, "O wretched man!" but with him likewise I can say, "I thank God through "Jesus Christ my Lord." I live in a barren land, where the knowledge and power of the gospel is very low; yet here are a few of the Lord's people; and this wilderness has been a useful school to me, where I have studied more leisurely the truths I gathered up in London. I brought down with

with me a confiderable ftock of notional truth, but I have fince found, that there is no effectual teacher but God; that we can receive no farther than he is pleafed to communicate; and that no knowledge is truly ufeful to me, but what is made my own by experience. Many things I thought I had learned, would not ftand in an hour of temptation, till I had in this way learned them over again. Since the year 1757, I have had an increafing acquaintance in the Weft-riding of Yorkfhire, where the gofpel flourifhes greatly. This has been a good fchool to me: I have converfed at large among all parties, without joining any; and in my attempts to hit the *golden mean*, I have fometimes been drawn too near the different extremes; yet the Lord has enabled me to profit by my miftakes. In brief, I am ftill a learner, and the Lord ftill condefcends to teach me. I begin at length to fee that I have attained but very little; but I truft in him to carry on his own work in my foul, and by all the difpenfations of his grace and providence, to increafe my knowledge of him, and of myfelf.

When I was fixed in a houfe, and found my

my business would afford me much leisure time, I considered in what manner I should improve it. And now having reason to close with the apostle's determination, "to know nothing but Jesus Christ and him crucified," I devoted my life to the prosecution of spiritual knowledge, and resolved to pursue nothing but in subservience to this main design. This resolution divorced me (as I have already hinted) from the classics and mathematics. My first attempt was to learn so much Greek, as would enable me to understand the New Testament and Septuagint; and when I had made some progress this way, I entered upon the Hebrew the following year; and two years afterwards, having surmised some advantages from the Syriac version, I began with that language. You must not think that I have attained, or ever aimed at a critical skill in any of these: I had no business with them, but as in reference to something else. I never read one classic author in the Greek; I thought it too late in life to take such a round in this language, as I had done in the Latin. I only wanted the signification of scriptural words and phrases, and for this I thought I might

avail

avail myself of *Scapula*, the *Synopsis*, and others, who had sustained the drudgery before me. In the Hebrew, I can read the historical books and psalms, with tolerable ease; but in the prophetical and difficult parts, I am frequently obliged to have recourse to *lexicons*, &c. However, I know so much, as to be able, with such helps as are at hand, to judge for myself the meaning of any passage I have occasion to consult. Beyond this I do not think of proceeding, if I can find better employment; for I would rather be some way useful to others, than die with the reputation of an eminent linguist.

Together with these studies, I have kept up a course of reading of the best writers in divinity that have come to my hand, in the Latin and English tongues, and some French, (for I picked up the French at times, while I used the sea). But within these two or three years, I have accustomed myself chiefly to writing, and have not found time to read many books besides the scriptures.

I am the more particular in this account, as my case has been something singular; for in all my literary attempts, I have been

obliged

obliged to strike out my own path, by the light I could acquire from books, as I have not had a teacher or assistant since I was ten years of age.

One word concerning my views to the *ministry*, and I have done.——I have told you, that this was my dear mother's hope concerning me; but her death, and the scenes of life in which I afterwards engaged, seemed to cut off the probability. The first desires of this sort in my own mind, arose many years ago, from a reflection on *Gal.* i. 23. 24. " But they had " heard only, That he which persecuted us " in times past, now preacheth the faith " which once he destroyed. And they glo- " rified God."——I could not but wish for such a public opportunity to testify the riches of divine grace. I thought I was, above most living, a fit person to proclaim that faithful saying, " That Jesus Christ " came into the world to save the chief of " sinners:" and as my life had been full of remarkable turns, and I seemed selected to shew what the Lord could do, I was in some hopes that, perhaps, sooner or later, he might call me into this service.

I believe it was a distant hope of this
that

that determined me to study the original scriptures; but it remained an imperfect desire in my own breast, till it was recommended to me by some Christian friends. I started at the thought when first seriously proposed to me; but afterwards set apart some weeks to consider the case, to consult my friends, and to entreat the Lord's direction—The judgment of my friends, and many things that occurred, tended to engage me. My first thought was to join the dissenters, from a presumption that I could not honestly make the required subscriptions; but Mr C——, in a conversation upon these points, moderated my scruples; and preferring the established church in some other respects, I accepted a title from him some months afterwards, and sollicited ordination from the late archbishop of York: I need not tell you I met a refusal, nor what steps I took afterwards to succeed elsewhere. At present I desist from my applications. My desire to serve the Lord is not weakened; but I am not so hasty to push myself forward as I was formerly. It is sufficient that he knows how to dispose of me, and that he both can and will do what is best. To him

I commend myself: I trust that his will and my true interest are inseparable. To his name be glory for ever. And thus I conclude my story, and presume you will acknowledge I have been particular enough. I have room for no more, but to repeat that

I am,

Sir,

February 2. 1763.

Yours, J. NEWTON.

A

DISCOURSE*

ON

1 TIMOTHY i. 15.

This is a faithful saying, and worthy of all acceptation, that Christ Jesus came into the world to save sinners; of whom I am chief.

THOUGH the apostle Paul has wrote largely and happily upon every branch of Christian doctrine and practice; and with respect to his writings, as well as his preaching, could justly assert, " that he had not shunned to declare the " whole counsel of God;" yet there are two points which seem to have been (if I may so speak) his favourite topics; which he most frequently repeats, most copiously insists on, and takes every occasion of in-

* By the author of the *Authentic Narrative.* J. Newton

P troducing

troducing. The one is, to display the honours, power, and faithfulness of the Lord Jesus Christ; the other, to make known the great things God had done for his own soul. How his heart was filled and fired with the first of these, is evident from almost every chapter of his Epistles. When he speaks of that mystery of godliness, "God manifested in the flesh," and the exceeding grace and love declared to a lost world through him, the utmost powers of language fall short of his purpose. With a noble freedom, he soars beyond the little bounds of criticism; and, finding the most expressive words too weak and faint for his ideas, he forms and compounds new ones; heaps one hyperbole upon another: yet, after his most laboured essays to do justice to his subject, he often breaks off in a manner that shews he was far from being satisfied with all he could say. This reflection is most obvious to those who can read him in the *original;* but no disadvantages of a translation can wholly confine that inimitable ardour with which he seems to pour his whole soul into his words, when he is speaking of his Lord and Saviour. And he who can read the first chapters of

his

his epistles to the Ephesians, Colossians, and Hebrews; the second to the Philippians, or many similar passages, with indifference, must be, I say, not merely a person of small devotion, but of little taste and sensibility.

And how deeply his mind was impressed with the mercies he had received in his conversion and call, is equally conspicuous. He takes every occasion to aggrandize the goodness of God to himself; to exaggerate and deplore the guilt and misery of his former life, in which he once trusted; and to lament the small returns he was able to make for such blessings; even when he could say, without boasting, that he had " laboured more abundantly" than the most diligent and zealous of his fellow-servants.

A powerful, abiding sense of these two points, upon the apostle's mind, have given rise to many sudden, lively, and beautiful digressions in the course of his writings. The context to the passage I have read, is of this kind. Having incidentally spoken of the gospel in the 11th verse, he is suddenly struck with the reflection of his own misery while ignorant of it, and the wonderful goodness of God, in affording him the knowledge of salvation, and honouring him (who was before a blasphemer) with a commission to publish the same glad tidings to others. This thought suspends his argument, and fills his heart and mouth with praise. And having acknowledged, that " the grace of our Lord " was exceeding abundant" towards himself, he subjoins the words of the text for an encouragement to others; assuring us that his case was not so peculiar, but that multitudes might be partakers with him in the same hope of mercy.

The words easily resolve into two parts.

First, A short, but comprehensive proposition, including the purport of the whole gospel; " that Jesus Christ came into the " world to save sinners."

Second, A commendation of this doctrine in a twofold respect; as " a faithful say- " ing," and as " worthy of all accepta- " tion." Each of these illustrated by the instance of himself; when he adds, ". of " whom I am chief."

The apostle well knew the different reception the gospel would meet in the world : that many poor, guilty souls,

trembling

trembling under a sense of sin and unworthiness, would very hardly be persuaded that such sinners as they could be saved at all. To these he recommends it as "a "faithful saying," founded upon the immutable counsel, promise, and oath of God, that Jesus Christ came into the world to save *sinners:* sinners in general; *the chief of sinners*, such as he represents himself to have been. He knew likewise, that many others, from a mistaken opinion of their own goodness, or a mistaken dependance on something of their own chusing, would be liable to undervalue this faithful saying. For the sake of these, he adds, it is "wor- "thy of all acceptation." None are so bad but the gospel affords them a ground of hope: none are so good, as to have any just ground of hope without it. There was a time when St Paul could have made a fair profession of himself likewise: he could say *, " circumcised on the eighth " day, of the stock of Israel, of the tribe " of Benjamin, an Hebrew of the Hebrews, " as to the law a Pharisee, as to the righ- " teousness which is by the law, blame- " less." But he has been since taught to

* Philip. iii.

count

count all things but loss for the excellency of the knowledge of Christ; and is content to style himself *the chief of sinners.*

Having thus attempted to shew the design and meaning of the words; I propose, something more at large, to unfold the proposition; and point out some of those important and extensive truths it contains. I say, *some of them;* for it is not possible, that either men or angels can fully sound the depth of this one sentence, " that Je-" sus Christ came into the world to save " sinners." I shall afterwards *infer* and *inforce* the other part of the text; that " it is *indeed* a faithful saying, and worthy " of all acceptation." And may He who came into the world to procure salvation for sinners, and is now exalted on high to bestow it, accompany the whole with his promised blessing.

The tenor of the proposition readily suggests three inquiries. 1*st*, Who this person is, here spoken of, Jesus Christ. 2*d*, What is meant by the salvation he is said to have undertaken. 3*d*, By what means he effected it.

Let us, *first*, speak of this gracious, this wonderful person, Jesus Christ. We already

ready bear his name as professed Christians; and we speak of him as *our Master*, and *our Lord;* and so far we say well. But, as he has told us, many will call him *Lord*, at the great day, to whom he will profess, " I never knew you, whence you are, de-" part:" so, it is to be feared, there are many *now*, that outwardly acknowledge him, who neither know *whence* he is, nor *who* he is: though we have Moses and the prophets, the apostles and evangelists, continually with us; though it is the immediate aim and intent of all their writings, in every history, promise, prophecy, type, ceremony and law, to set *him* before our eyes; and though there is hardly an image in the material creation, but is adopted by the scriptures to shadow forth his excellency. Ignorance of Jesus Christ, and what he has done for his people, is the great cause that religion appears so *low* and *contemptible* to some, and is found so *tedious* and *burthensome* by others. Let us therefore attend " to the record God has given " of his Son:" for I propose, in this article, to say little of my own; but to lay before you the express, powerful, indubitable testimony of holy scripture.

And

And here we are taught, 1*st*, *That Jesus Christ is God.* The first words of St John's gospel are full to this point. " In the be-" ginning;" that is, at the commencement of time and things, when as yet nothing else existed, " was the Word, and the Word " was with God, and the Word was God *." To prevent a possibility of mistake, and to confirm the eternity of this divine Word in the strongest manner, it is immediately added, " the same was in the beginning " with God. All things were made by him." And, lest this likewise should be either contested or misunderstood, it is guarded by an universal negative; " without him " was not any thing made that was made." Further, to prevent (if possible) the surmise, that, in these glorious works, the eternal Word acted with a deputed power only, the apostle subjoins, " in him was " life;" life essentially; and, from him as the fountain, life and light proceeded to his creatures: " in him was life, and that " life was the light of men." To this agrees the declaration of St Paul †, " for " by him were all things created that are " in heaven, and that are in earth; visible

* John i. † Colloss. i.

" or

"or invisible; whether thrones, or domi-
"nions, or principalities, or powers; all
"things were created by him, and for
"him:" *by* his power and wisdom, *for* his
glory and pleasure. "And he is before
"all things, and by him all things consist."
Elsewhere he speaks of him expressly, as
"over all, God blessed for ever; who up-
"holdeth all things by the word of his
"power; the same yesterday, to-day and
"for ever. It were easy to enlarge this
way; but I shall content myself with observing this general proof of the divinity of Christ, that the scriptures, which were given to make us wise to salvation, do ascribe to him the names of God, particularly JEHOVAH; the essential attributes of God, such as Eternity, Omnipresence, Omnipotence; the peculiar works of God, as Creation, Providence, Redemption, and Forgiveness of sin; and finally, commands us to pay him those *divine* honours, and to rely on him with that *absolute dependence*, which would be idolatry, if referred any where below the supreme Majesty of heaven and earth.

Again, we learn from scripture, that Christ is truly and properly *man*. This is indeed wonderful! therefore styled "the "great mystery of godliness *. But that he, of whom we have begun to speak, is the very person who came into the world to save sinners, we have abundant proof. The apostle John, whose testimony we have already cited, says, a few verses lower †, "and the Word," that glorious word, which was God with God, "was made "flesh, and dwelt amongst us, and we be-"held his glory," that is, we his disciples, whose eyes were spiritually enlightened, (for the world in general saw nothing of it), as the glory of "the only be-"gotten of the Father, full of grace and "truth." In other places it is said, "Him-"self took our infirmities, and bore our "sicknesses; and was in all points tempt-"ed as we are, yet without sin ‡. As the "children are partakers of flesh and blood, "he also, himself, likewise took part of "the same ||. In the fulness of time, God "sent forth his Son, made of a woman +." Many are the mistakes of mortals; and wide the extremes into which mistaken mortals run! Some have rashly ventured

* 1 Tim. iii. † John i. ‡ Isa. liii. || Heb. iv. 15. ii. 14. + Gal. iv.

to

to deny our Lord's divinity: some have wildly and fancifully explained away his humanity: but may we (through grace) abide by the scriptural truth, and be directed in the midst of the path of judgment.

From this mystical union of the divine and human nature in one person, the scriptures speak of him, *thirdly*, under the character of a *Mediator:* " the one Mediator between God and man." To this idea, the names JESUS CHRIST, which are as ointment poured forth, direct us in their original import. The former, which signifies the *Saviour*, pointing out the success and efficacy of his undertaking; the latter, which is the same with *Messiah*, or the *Anointed*, expressing both his divine appointment thereto, and the compleat supply of all grace and power, wherewith he was filled for the discharge of it. Thus much for the person spoken of.

We proceed, in the *next* place, to consider the design of his appearance in the world: " To save sinners." And, as the idea of *deliverance* presupposes a state of *distress*, it will be necessary previously to inquire into the condition of those whom

he

he came to save; which is indeed emphatically implied in the appellation given them, *sinners*. Man, having broke that law under which he was created, and with which his happiness was closely connected, fell under accumulated ruin. The image of God, in which he was formed, was defaced, and a far different image set up in his heart; even of him who had seduced him from his allegiance: darkness in the understanding, rebellion in the will, sensuality in the affections. The justice of God threatning a penalty he could neither satisfy nor sustain. The commandments of God still challenging an obedience he had no longer any power to yield. The very gifts and bounties of God, with which he was encompassed, designed not only for his comfort, but his instruction, to lead him, as by so many steps, to their gracious author, became, eventually, the occasions of withdrawing him farther from his duty, and increasing, as well as aggravating his ingratitude. Thus stood man towards his Maker. With regard to his fellow-creatures; self-love and inordinate desires, having raised a variety of interfering interests in the breasts

of

of all, peace withdrew from the earth: every man's heart and hand was set against his neighbour, and violence, rage, envy, and confusion overspread the world. Nor could he be easier in himself: hurried by restless desires towards things either unsatisfying or unattainable; haunted with cares, tortured with pains, tired with opposition, shocked with disappointment. Conscience, like the hand that appeared in Belshazzar's feast*, writing bitter things against him, when outward circumstances allowed a short repose; and vanity, like a worm, destroying the root of every flower that promised the fairest bloom of success. Behold a few outlines of the picture of fallen man! Miserable in his life; more miserable in the continual dread of losing *such* a life; miserable most of all, that neither his fancy can feign, nor his fear conceive the consequences of the death he dreads; which will introduce him to the immediate presence, to the *tribunal* of an incensed, almighty, ever-living God!

Such was the state from which Jesus Christ came to save us. He came to restore us to the favour of God, to reconcile

* Daniel v. 5.

us to ourselves, and to each other; to give us peace and joy in life, hope and triumph in death, and after death; glory, honour, and immortality. For he came not merely to repair and to reſtore, but to exalt: not only " that we might have life," the life we had forfeited, but " that we might " have it more abundantly *." That our happineſs might be more exalted, our title more firm, and our poſſeſſion more ſecure than the ſtate of Adam in paradiſe could boaſt, or than his poſterity could have attained unto, if he had continued unſinning upon the tenor of the firſt covenant.

Now, could we ſuppoſe it poſſible that a ſet of innocent beings, without any default of their own, had ſunk into a ſtate of miſery, we muſt confeſs it would have been great grace and favour in the Lord Jeſus to ſave them. But let us not forget the ſtreſs laid in the text upon the word *ſinners*. He came to ſave, not the unfortunate, but the *ungodly* †. How then ſhould every heart glow with love to him, who hath thus loved us! If any of *us* can hear or ſpeak of this ſubject with indifference or diſguſt, it is to be feared we are quite

* John x. 10. † Rom. v. 6.

ſtrangers

strangers to the *nature*, or the *necessity*, of that salvation with which God has graciously visited his people. Let us no more usurp the sacred words of generosity, sensibility, or gratitude, if this astonishing instance of divine goodness leaves us cold and unimpressed; especially if to this we join the consideration of the *third* point I proposed to speak of; by what means *Jesus Christ* effected this salvation for sinners.

In the passage before us, it is only said, that he " came into the world " on this account; which teacheth us, *this* was the sole design of his advent; and that, coming on set purpose for this, he would leave nothing undone that was necessary to accomplish it. He emptied himself of that divine glory and honour he possessed with the Father from eternity. " He bow-" ed the heavens, and came down " to our earth; and that not with an external glory, as a celestial messenger, to constrain the attention and homage of mankind, " but was made of a woman*;" not of high and noble extraction, in the judgment of men, " but in the form of a servant:" born in a stable; laid in a manger; brought up in an obscure and contemptible place,

* Gal. iv. 4.

and reputed no higher than the son of a carpenter. " He was despised and rejected " of men; there was no form of comeli- " ness in him *," to attract a general regard; on the contrary, " he came to his " own, and his own received him not †." Farther, as he was made of a woman, " he " was made under the law;" the one in order to the other: for this was the way divine wisdom had appointed, and which divine justice required, to make salvation possible to sinners. Eternal Truth had pronounced tribulation, wrath, and anguish, upon every soul of man that doth evil. All men, in every age and place, "had corrupt- " ed their ways before God;" yet his mercy had designed, that where sin had abounded, grace should much more abound ‡. Jesus Christ was the grand expedient, in whom " mercy and truth met together ‖;" and the inflexible *righteousness* of God was brought to correspond and harmonize with the peace of sinful man. That justice might be satisfied, truth vindicated, and sinners saved, " God so loved" a lost " world," when no inferior means could avail, none in heaven or earth were *will-*

iii. † John i. ‡ Rom. v. 20. ‖ Psal. lxxxv.

ing,

ing, or *worthy*, or *able*, to interpose, " he " gave his only begotten Son *." Jesus Christ, the brightness of the Father's glory, and the express image of his person, *so loved the world*, that he assumed our nature, undertook our cause, bore our sins, sustained our deserved punishment; and having done and suffered all that the case required, he is now gone before, *to prepare a place* † for all that believe in him and obey him. Man lay under a double incapacity for happiness; he could neither keep the law of God in future, nor satisfy for his past breach and contempt of it. To obviate the former, Jesus Christ performed a perfect, unsinning obedience in our stead. To remove the latter, he became " the pro- " pitiation of our sins;" yielded up his life as a prey into the hands of murderers, and poured forth his precious blood in drops of sweat in the garden, in streams from his side upon the cross. For this he endured the fiercest temptations of the devil, the scorn, rage, and malice of men, and drank the bitter cup of the wrath of God, when it pleased the Father to bruise him, and make his soul an offering for sin. His

* John iii. 16.   † John xiv. 2.

love carried him through all; and when he had finally overcome the sharpness of death, he opened the kingdom of heaven to all believers. In few words, he lived and died for us when upon earth, nor is he unmindful of us in heaven, but lives and intercedes on our behalf. He continually executes the offices of prophet, priest, and king to his people, instructing them by his word and Spirit, presenting their persons and prayers acceptable to God through his merits, defending them by his power from all their enemies, ghostly and bodily, and ordering, by his providence, all things to work together for their good, till at length they are brought home to be with him where he is, and to behold his glory.

From what has been said, we may justly infer, in the *first* place, " that this is," as the apostle styles it, " a faithful say-" ing." When man first fell, God, in the midst of judgment remembering mercy, declared, unsought and undesired, " that " the seed of the woman should bruise the " serpent's head *." In every succeeding age he confirmed his purpose by types,

* Genesis iii.

promises,

promises, prophecies and oaths. At length, in the fulness of time, Christ, "the desire "of all nations," came into the world, fulfilled all that had been foretold, and encouraged every humble penitent sinner to come unto him that they might have life, pardon and peace. To doubt or to deny his readiness to save, is, so far as in us lyes, to "make the word of God of "none effect;" it is "to charge God "foolishly," as though, like the heedless unskilful builder in the gospel, he had begun to build that which was not to be finished. If, after all that is set before us, it is possible for any soul to miss salvation that sincerely desires it, and seeks it in God's appointed way, it must be because the Lord Jesus Christ either *cannot*, or *will not* save them. That he cannot, is flatly false; for "all power is his in heaven and "in earth *;" and it is particularly said, that "he is able to save unto the uttermost "all that come unto God by him † :" and that he will not, is as false; for he himself hath said, "Whosoever cometh unto "me, I will in no wise cast out ‡."

We may infer, *secondly*, that this doc-

* Matth. xxviii. † Heb. vii. ‡ John vi.

trine is not only faithful, but "worthy of "all acceptation." And here methinks I could begin anew: a point so much mistaken by some, and neglected by most, rather requires a whole, or many discourses, than to be passed over in a few words. The most high and wise God has esteemed the redemption of mankind so precious, "that he spared not his only Son *."——— And are there any amongst us, in a land of gospel-light and liberty, where the words of wisdom are sounding in our ears every day, that dare make light of this message? just give it a hearing, and return to their farms, their merchandise, and their diversions, as though this unspeakable grace of God called for no return? Alas! "how "shall we escape if we neglect this salva-"tion †? He that despised Moses' law died "without mercy." It was dangerous, it was destructive to refuse him that spoke upon earth; take heed how you trifle with him "that speaketh from heaven!" To such as neglect this, "there remains no "other sacrifice for sin; but a certain "fearful looking for of fiery indignation, "that shall devour the adversaries ‡" Let

* Rom. viii.   † Heb. ii. 3.   ‡ Heb. x. 26. 27.

none

none of us think it is well with us merely because we were born and educated in a Christian country, have means of instruction in our hands, and enjoy frequent opportunities of presenting ourselves before God in public worship. To thousands these, so far from being advantages, will greatly aggravate their condemnation, and point the sting of the never-dying worm. Better were it for us to have been inhabitants of Tyre and Sidon *, yea, of Sodom and Gomorrah, than to appear in judgment with no better plea than this. Neither let us speak peace to ourselves, because we are not so bad as others, but perhaps live decently, and comfortably, are useful in society, and perform many things that are commonly called *good works*. If these works spring from a true love of God, if they are framed according to the rule of his word, if they are performed by faith in Christ Jesus our Lord, they are undoubtedly good, and shall be rewarded before men and angels; if otherwise, you have already your reward, in the complacence of your own minds, and the approbation of friends and acquaintance. The Christianity of the New Testament imports more than all this.

* Luke x. 13.

It is to believe in Jesus Christ; so to believe in him, as to obey him in all his commands; to trust him in all his dispensations; to walk in his steps, copying out the bright example of his love, meekness, patience, self-denial, and active zeal for the glory of God and the good of mankind.——It is, from a consciousness of our utter inability to perform these great things, to depend continually upon the promised aid and direction of his holy Spirit; to seek this assistance by frequent fervent prayer, to offer up ourselves daily as living sacrifices unto God.——And, finally, when we have done all, to be deeply sensible of our unworthiness of the least of his mercies; to confess ourselves unprofitable servants; and to place all our hopes upon this faithful saying, " that Jesus " Christ came into the world to save sin- " ners."

Thus, from the consideration of the person of the Lord Jesus Christ, the greatness of our misery by nature, and the wonderful things he has done and suffered for our redemption, we may learn, the compleat security of that salvation he has provided; the extreme danger of neglecting it, and he folly and presumption of attempting

to

to establish a righteousness of our own, independent of him, "who is appointed "of God unto us, wisdom, righteousness, "sanctification, and redemption *." In setting these things before you plainly and faithfully, I trust I have delivered my own soul. Time is short, life is precarious, and perhaps to some this may be the last opportunity of the kind that may be afforded them. God grant we may be wise in time, "that to day, while it is called "To-day," we may hear his voice. Then we shall understand more of the text than words can teach us; then we shall experience "a peace that passeth all under- "standing †, a joy which a stranger in- "termedleth not with ‡," and a hope "full of glory," which shall be compleated in the endless possession of those "plea- "sures which are at the right hand of "God ‖;" where sin, and its inseparable attendant sorrow, shall cease for ever; where "there shall be no more grief, or "pain, or fear ††;" but every tear shall be wiped from every eye.

* 2 Cor. i. † Philip. iv. ‡ Prov. xiv. ‖ Psal. xvi. †† Rev. xxi.

F I N I S.

Books just published.

The Communicant's Spiritual Companion; or, An evangelical Preparation for the LORD's Supper. By the Rev. Thomas Haweis. Price 2 s.

The Mourner; or, The afflicted relieved. By Benjamin Grosvenor, D. D. Price 1 s. 8 d.

Social Religion exemplified, in an account of the first settlement of Christianity in the city of Caerludd; in several dialogues. The third edition. Price 6 s.

The Governess; or, The history of Mrs Teachum and her nine girls. Price 1 s. 6 d.

Magazin des Enfans: or, The young Misses Magazine. Containing dialogues between a Governess and several young Ladies of quality her scholars, 2 vols. Price 5 s.

Nature and Grace; or, Some essential differences between the sentiments of the natural and spiritual. The third edition. Price 1 d. or 10 d. the dozen.